THE ART OF LOOKING INTO THE FUTURE

R.S. AMBLEE

THE ART OF LOOKING INTO THE FUTURE

THE FIVE PRINCIPLES OF TECHNOLOGICAL EVOLUTION

GLOTURE BOOKS

This book may be ordered through booksellers or by contacting the publisher.

www.gloturebooks.com

Grateful acknowledgment is made to the following for permission to reprint excerpts of their work: International Monetary Fund, Dow Jones and Company, Inc., *World Health Organization*, *The National Center for Public Policy and Higher Education,* www.House.gov, www.cbo.gov, www.eia.doe.gov, www.nasa.gov, www.ers.usda.gov, www.oecd.org and www.cms.gov.

ISBN-10: 0983157405
EAN-13: 9780983157403

GLOTURE BOOKS

Contents

INTRODUCTION

Looking into the future does not come naturally for most of us. In fact, it is hard enough for us to see past today! This book makes an effort to present a technique for looking into the future with real world examples. Together we will journey into a fascinating future and see our own life. As we travel together, we will notice all of the technological marvels of the future are inevitable because the human technological evolution is unstoppable. We will explore how human life will change and how future generations must be prepared to face it.

During our discussion, we will not make unrealistic assumptions the world will experience some extraordinary technological breakthroughs, but rather will use whatever technology we have today – and more toil and sweat – at the research table to discover the inevitability of human progress.

Though our ancestors built highways and mega bridges with an expectation of a better future, they could see only a near future and not a distant one. They could not see the world centuries into the future. The energy crisis is one such example. With industries built around oil and coal, our ancestors possibly knew that one day these resources would not be able to support the huge global demand. However, they did not know it would arrive so soon. They never imagined underdeveloped countries would progress so fast. They were simply not able to estimate the size of today's global economy from the vantage point of those long-forgotten "good old days."

The one guideline I use extensively in this book, and will continue to use in future work, is to look at our history, not just for facts but also for a pattern.

This search for a predictable paradigm in human history is highly intuitive and provokes thoughts of futuristic possibilities. It allows us to develop forward-thinking capabilities and possible ways to predict the future of technological evolution.

PART 1

The Fundamentals

IN THIS PART:

CHAPTER 1

THE JOURNEY SO FAR

RESTLESS THOUGHTS

Ever since the proverbial sky began falling on poor Chicken Little, we have been hearing nearly endless scientific theories of how the world will end. Now, more than ever, most of those theories feature the devastating forces of black holes, gamma rays, asteroid strikes, global warming, and a nonstop list of other extinction level threats straight out of last summer's million-dollar blockbuster films.

Unfortunately for our species, the list of dangers to our survival keeps growing as we find new technologies that discover hidden threats to humanity. From all outward indications, human beings are so fragile we do not stand a chance against such global disasters. Considering the grave nature of those considerable forces working against us, it is extremely fortunate we have survived for so long without becoming extinct.

While intellectuals who understand these very real, very scientific, and very provable threats feel understandably helpless, the public seems to pay little attention to the daily indicators of our impending doom. To them, it seems such stories more closely resemble grandma's bedtime fairytales of old – a little fantasy, a little folly – quickly forgotten in the night's other restless thoughts. To the public eye, those threats attract the same attention as any other daily news.

MASS EXTINCTION?

Protecting ourselves from any of these disasters is so unfeasible it would take billions of dollars to even investigate and understand the nature of those issues we face, let alone blueprint and implement them. Even though our technology appears to be advancing at a dizzying speed, when it comes to finding authentic solutions to these credible threats, we still have a long way to go.

Our governments cannot initiate any type of decisive action until there is sufficient proof to convince the majority in the legislature to use public money to achieve such means. Private businesses, which are under no such restrictions, shy away from entering into the fray, because the investments are still too risky to consider seriously.

So, what is to be our fate as a species, as a race of people, of individuals, of communities…as a planet? Will we all become helpless victims of mass extinction?

There is only one answer to this question: **It all depends on where we are along our technological evolutionary path when we encounter those threats**. Ideally, we will be at the right level of technological evolution to survive certain extinction-level threats. If we encounter them prematurely, before we have sufficiently evolved to withstand them, we may not stand a chance.

On the other hand, if those threats come at a later stage, *after* we cross that evolutional demarcation point, we will not only survive, but also alter those situations to our advantage and indeed flourish in the coming age(s) of our existence.

Solar flares, as an example, are a threat to our ecosystem, but evolution creates strengths out of weaknesses. Imagine the ramifications if we could harness the sun's tremendous amount of energy. Technological evolution will make it so.

Volcanoes, forest fires, hurricanes, and tornados are all examples of huge energy losses we are unable to capture because of our current technological inadequacies. Instead, we run away from such energy sources, because we are simply not there yet along our evolutionary timeline.

WE HAVE A NATURAL DESIRE TO EVOLVE TECHNOLOGICALLY

Unlike animals that are forced to adapt physically to changing environments for survival, as human beings we bring that change upon ourselves by discovering new technologies through intellectual ability and adaptation to a higher standard of living. Rather than experiencing the hormonal "fight or flight" response of wild animals, we experience "spy it and buy it" instead.

Humans seem to have an almost insatiable desire to acquire "things" to lead a safer and easier, often upscale life. Even extremely wealthy people, who have all the creature comforts in the world, look for innovative items in the market to make their lives even better. The wealthy and elite are usually the first ones to buy new hi-tech, and high priced, gadgets when they arrive on the market. What is behind this craze for better living? Why are we not happy with what we have?

The answer to this question is in our natural desire to evolve technologically. We contribute to this natural evolution on a daily basis. Suppose you are in a wine shop looking for a particular vintage. Say you stumble upon a new design of bottle opener in your search for the perfect Pinot Noir. You wish to own it and get excited about buying it, even though you already have several bottle openers at home, all of which are more than sufficient for the job. The only things that may stop you from making the purchase are the **quality and price**. If the price is within your budget and the quality is acceptable to you, you will go for it. This natural desire is always toward the next big thing – the next level of technology – to make life easier.

It is not simply mass production or low price attracting us; it is our **desire** to have new tools to make our lives easier. That is what has moved this evolutionary process to where it stands today. Every day we try to make life better than yesterday. This natural desire brought us out of Stone Age caves to present day luxury living.

CONSUMERISM, NOT NECESSITY, IS THE MOTHER OF ALL INVENTIONS

Consumerism is what makes inventions successful. If a great innovation comes to the market but no one is interested in buying it, it is worthless. We give credit to great inventors for improving our lives immeasurably, but forget the end-users who created the demand for the product in the first place. For example, Thomas Edison is widely remembered as the inventor of the electric light bulb. What if no one wanted to use electricity and we were all just as happy with candlesticks and fireplaces? Without end-users to clamor for his brainstorm, like so many before or since, that invention would have vanished into thin air, along with Edison's estimable legacy.

Instead, the light bulb became a big success because of the common person's desire to use that technology to achieve a higher standard of living. Candles, matches, flames, and candleholders evolved to light bulbs, fixtures, light switches, and remote controls. As long as this desire to improve our lives continually exists, **human technological evolution simply cannot be stopped**. Inventors' innovative ideas are absorbed by the commercial market as quickly as they appear, although not all inventions are successful.

Even though intellectual efforts are important, the truth is, even if those scientists were never born, someone else would have created those inventions later. Human evolutionary activity is a collective effort and does not bear adherence to any one individual. The technological evolution is as natural as human life. Regardless of how consciously we consider it (if at all), we are all part of this natural process.

SLOW AND STEADY WINS THE (HUMAN) RACE

If, on the other hand, an innovation were too futuristic for current times, it would remain on the back burner until its day finally arrived. Evolutionary changes have to be slow and steady to match the absorption capacity of the market; it takes time for people to adapt to these changes. For example, some of the inventions of Leonardo da Vinci never saw the light of the day during his own lifetime or for centuries later. They remained on paper all the time waiting, in effect, for history to catch up with the great inventor. Now, after so many centuries, scientists are able to analyze and understand what he was trying to bring to life.

The same argument goes for many of Einstein's theories, from the theory of relativity to dark matter. Some theories are even too futuristic for us to understand today, let alone consider using them in our products. As human knowledge advances, however, those futuristic concepts will be verified and eventually absorbed into the system. Until then, sadly, they will remain on the evolutional back burner until we as a species catch up to them.

CHAPTER 2

UNDERSTANDING TECHNOLOGICAL EVOLUTION

THE PLEASURE AND THE PAIN

Human technological evolution is a process of discovering new technologies to satisfy human desires. It is not just the invention but the consumption as well. Throughout this book, the discussion focuses on ***technological evolution***, not ***biological evolution***. Henceforth, use of the term "evolution" refers to technological evolution.

All the present high-tech marvels we enjoy today – from smart phones to laptops to whisper quiet washing machines – exist because of the many geniuses throughout modern history that devoted their lives to inventions. Humans have responded positively by encouraging such inventions, either by buying them or investing in them.

Not all inventions become successful. Only some become very popular and even become mega industries employing thousands of people.

New ideas fail, if the product or service is not competitive, in either price or quality, or if they are simply not inspiring enough for people to buy them. This is the reason why thousands of new inventions vanish before they hit the market. The market absorbs only those technologies that are affordable and improve consumers' standard of living. Surprisingly, the failure of certain inventions does not affect the evolutionary process. Instead, new companies/businesses keep popping up and the competition for survival continues.

Depending on which section of the human population a particular invention targets, the price and quality must be right for it to succeed. Obviously, this process of natural selection leaves many new inventions out in the cold.

Comparing the number of utility products in our homes today to what people had 100 years ago is staggering. By encouraging these products, we have come a long way in creating a web of industries and an enormous global economy that sustains, comforts, feeds, and enriches us on a daily basis.

Consumers always look for less expensive but higher quality products, and throughout commercial history, businesses have always competed with each other to produce them. This partnership between producer and consumer is the backbone of human technological evolution. We evolved to our present state on this model and we will continue evolving on it into the future.

The technological evolution has not come without problems. Employees are at a higher stress level than just a few decades ago. Many employees work several hours beyond their forty-hour-a-week limits to meet the crushing deadlines that are now a daily reality in order to produce products faster and cheaper.

Employees not only work harder every day but also have to increase productivity to reduce the overhead to the company; multi-tasking to increase efficiency on behalf of their employer is now a job within a job. Every day employees have to prove they are still the best and make the company highly competitive in the market. If not, they will be replaced quickly, for the simple reason companies cannot afford to keep less skilled workers on the payroll when others will do the job more quickly or efficiently. After all, if they do, they will lose out to the competition.

If we examine it from an evolutionary standpoint, this complicated employee-employer partnership bears a close resemblance to the "survival of the fittest" theory. Those who adapt, will survive; those who do not, will perish.

Why do we make our lives so stressful? Again, the answer to this question is in our natural desire to evolve. Humans have an intense desire to evolve so we are all equally responsible for such hardship. As an illustration, every time you shop for a less expensive product in a shopping mall or major department store, you are unknowingly responsible for creating competition in the marketplace. The act of choosing a less expensive product over a more expensive one could potentially bankrupt a less competitive business or cause the lay-off of a less skilled employee. Many of us are unable to correlate the two, though there is a distinct relationship between them to even the most casual of observers.

Every time we go to a supermarket and pick a less expensive item of equal or superior quality as opposed to a more expensive one, we are indirectly responsible for putting stress on the employees that produce the more expensive item. Thus, the cheaper we buy, the more competitive those companies become. There is immense pressure on employees, as well as employers, to survive in this competitive economy, despite the fact we are all proud to live in such a civilized world.

This "human technological evolution" is unstoppable and its consequences are inevitable.

DISCOURAGING COMPETITION, FOR BETTER OR WORSE

Many countries have tried a different route to stem the tide of this blistering competitive marketplace and its effect on their economies. They have made regulations that discourage outside competition. They have insulated their local industries by not allowing outside products. Despite their best efforts, however, this fiscal protection for the local enterprisers and a stringent sense of job security for the employees over a long period has resulted in their economy lagging behind the rest of the world.

Lack of competition gives no motivation for businesses to grow. It will be inevitable that those governments will open their doors to world competition, so not only their local businesses will capture the world market but also invite global investments. It is a well-known fact an open economy is the fastest way to grow and the only way to survive in the real world. Every business is competing with the rest of the world; there is no "time out" for the competitive retailer.

Today, of course, many businesses are becoming global on day one. Internet e-commerce has made this happen with a technological evolution that has been both steep and unforgiving; seemingly, overnight the industrial world entered unblinkingly into the Information Age. Any successful invention quickly becomes a global product, thanks to the Internet; adapt or perish is once again the new battle cry for companies wishing to compete and, naturally, survive.

CHAPTER 3

THE NEED TO LOOK AT THE FUTURE

CURRENT ENERGY BOTTLENECK

To endure in this competitive market, industries need three important resources: inexpensive **R**aw materials, inexpensive **E**nergy, and inexpensive **L**abor (or **REL** for short) to lower their cost of production. As long as **REL** is low, the final product is less expensive.

In many industries, technology also adds to the cost of the product or services. For example, in the pharmaceutical industry, the cost of research substantially adds to the cost of the product. However, if you look at research as part of the industry, then the cost of research work represents the cost of skilled labor force. (In this book, when referring to **REL**, it includes the labor investment to develop technology.)

Although many times, raw materials and labor pose problems and increase the cost of the product, industries quickly find alternative solutions to solve the problem. For example, if wood and steel become prohibitively expensive because of a sudden shortage, industries will quickly replace them with alternative materials like plastic, rubber, or other alloys. Having already gone through the plastic era in our lifetime, we have witnessed how plastic rapidly replaced many traditional raw materials. Though it is not a permanent solution, this "band-aid" quickly became an easy fix. Industries continually look for and research alternative materials to make a product cheaper and/or with better quality to win in the competitive marketplace.

Similarly, if labor becomes expensive in one area of the world, industries hire labor from other areas in the region. To make products cheaper and to survive in global competition, businesses are constantly looking for low cost labor, not at a national level, but at a global level. The eventual result of this labor fickleness is, of course, the dreaded "outsourcing" that robs employees in one country/state while rewarding employees somewhere else, often a world away.

Outsourcing started a few years ago, with developed countries looking for low cost labor in less developed countries. This outsourcing has helped develop those countries as well. The standard of living in many less developed countries has increased due to this. Many countries that used to provide low cost labor are also becoming more expensive. Industries in developed countries will continue to hunt for even lower cost labor elsewhere.

The most important factor in the **REL** resource group is energy, which affects industries globally. When the economy grows at a steady pace, the increased demand for energy makes it expensive and, in turn, increases the cost of all goods and services. When that happens, the buying capacity of people decreases. This slows down the economy. This fluctuation in energy demand/supply is one of the major causes of economic boom and recession.

The graph below shows the world's continuously increasing energy consumption since 1775.

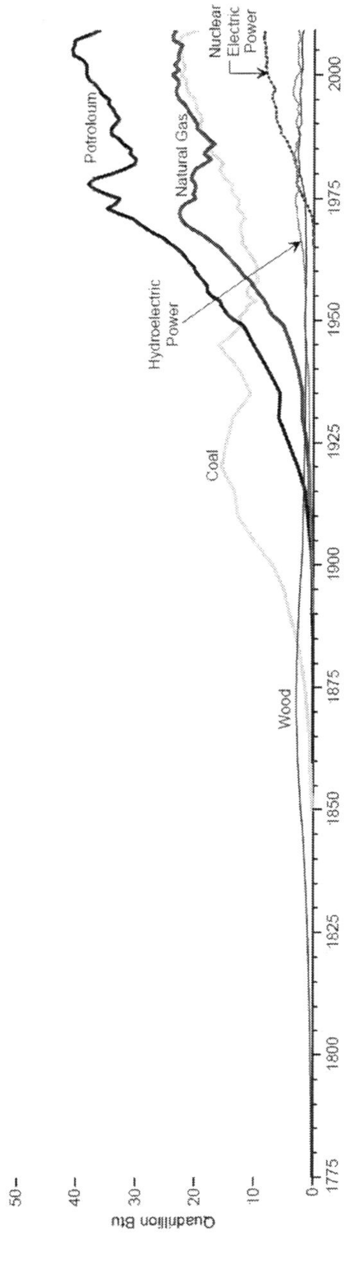

Fig-1: Primary Energy Consumption by Source 1775-2009, Source: U.S. Energy Information Administration, Annual Energy Review 2009: Energy Perspectives: 1949-2009 Report No. DOE/EIA-0384(2009): Release Date: August 19, 2010

Humans are depending on resources like coal and oil, which have huge production backlogs. For example, an oil refinery takes nearly a decade to complete a turnkey project from start to finish, which is far from an overnight answer to a very critical demand. With this kind of serious bottleneck in place, energy production always lags behind demand and quickly reaches the limit when demand exceeds supply during sudden, or even steady, economic growth.

The graph below shows the effect of energy bottleneck on the global economy in the near future. [Author's perception]

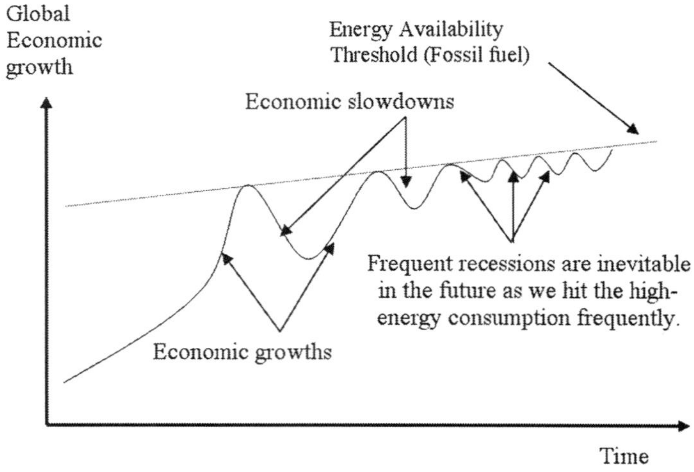

Fig-2: Future Energy Bottleneck

With this energy bottleneck, our technological evolution is like a bird learning to **fly**. Until its wing muscles become stronger, it keeps falling. Until we find a great source to produce energy, we will keep hitting this bottleneck and endure economic recessions.

Similar to energy bottleneck, there are many other factors that are responsible for economic recession. Every recession takes years to recover from and more than a decade to regain the lost momentum. The economy in US, Europe and other countries around the world has collapsed several times this century; this has been a painful experience for all of us.

IS THIS ECONOMIC GROWTH WORTH IT?

With the ebb and flow of our global economy, we see people expressing their concern about the future of the world, as we know it. Looking at all the stress people go through during the economic boom and subsequent suffering during the recession, it is natural for people to wonder, "Is this economic growth really worth it?"

The reality is there is no end to human desire; it only increases as our standard of living rises. A person with one television desires another; eventually those two televisions are not big enough, and so they replace them with two big-screens. Later, they may upgrade to high-definition. A person having one cell phone naturally wishes to have one for each family member. These are reasonable desires, considering our modern lifestyles. After all, as technology races ahead of demand, the products become increasingly affordable.

These desires are natural and inevitable as families, incomes, and even expectations grow. With an economy built on satisfying these desires, we have very little control over its growth. As technology brings advanced products to market, our desire to own them naturally increases. In fact, we work even harder to acquire them.

The other interesting aspect of human technological evolution is that growth is not linear. Sometimes it is very slow and other times it is visibly fast. When it is slow, we believe the world is going to be like this forever. Slow evolution places stress and frustration on us all. Despite working hard, it can take generations for families to rise out of poverty. Even education is not within their reach, nor was it for their ancestors. They do not believe they are evolving, though they are, in fact, part of the evolution.

Looking at the bigger picture of human evolutionary history, the facts are amazing. From the cave man's way of life to a modern luxury home is a colossal technological evolution. However, it took us a very long time. Now, we are slowly beginning to understand this pace is not arbitrary or subjective – the pace is in our own hands.

Though the human mind is extraordinarily intelligent, we often misunderstand each other. Our egos clash. Our emotions get the best of us, sapping our intellect and rationale. We let our greed take over. We have lived with these shortcomings since the day humans started thinking, feuding, envying, and betraying. These shortcomings have led to isolationism, territorialism and, occasionally, war and destruction. Technological evolution moves at a slow pace during difficult times. However, human technological evolution is an unstoppable process. Events like war and recession can slow it down or pause it for a while but cannot stop it. Its pace is entirely up to us; we can move at an amazing pace or pause it for a long time.

As long as we are weak, the chances of surviving global disasters are very bleak. Every day is important in our progress towards the strong future.

Since industrialization, the pace of technological evolution has increased dramatically. Our lives have changed noticeably, too. The changes the world faced in the past decade are significantly larger than any time in human history, with an exponential evolutionary pace.

If humans continue to evolve, what will our future look like? How far will our standard of living go? Will we ever be more capable of handling a coming global crisis like global warming or a meteor strike?

Though these thought-provoking questions seem impossible to answer now, by learning the "art of looking into the future," we can potentially visualize how humans can – and will – progress to meet the inevitable challenges and demands of the future.

THE ART OF LOOKING INTO THE FUTURE

"If we can contemplate how today evolved from yesterday, then we can see tomorrow."

It sounds so simple, yet there are no well-defined principles to make a start toward looking at that future. This book is all about establishing those basic principles to learn this skill. As we discuss and analyze these principles, we will more clearly see the obscure, hidden path and feel the strength of the evolutionary forces.

There are five fundamental principles needed to help us look into the future.

- The Principle of Desire
- The Principle of Globalization
- The Principle of Automation
- The Principle of Technological Evolution
- The Principle of Economic Recession

The next part discusses these principles in detail.

PART II

The Art of Looking into the Future

The Five Principles

IN THIS PART:

CHAPTER 4

THE PRINCIPLE OF DESIRE

THE DRIVING FORCE

Nothing moves in the world without a driving force. Human desire is the driving force behind all of our evolutionary activity. In fact, our daily actions and decisions revolve around this desire to want and get more.

We fail to notice many natural evolutionary behaviors even though they are with us constantly. For instance, when we go to a theater, we do not take just any seat. Instead, we will look for the best available seat from which we can get a better view of the stage. When we go to a restaurant, unless a staff member or host seats us, we will not take just any seat, but will look for a seat that gives more privacy or a better view of outside. Every step of the way, we try to make our life better.

This human desire is the driving force in our day-to-day actions and decisions, and is in the back of our mind all of the time. This force drives our technological evolution.

Every time we go shopping, we notice a host of new products. They are all products of intense human desire. The success of these products depends on how affordable they are and how much desire they satisfy for the end consumer, be it a new smart phone or a video game or, for that matter, a tote bag.

To understand this first principle of evolution, we need to focus on three basic criteria that show why products and services are invented and their future evolution. They are: **Invention/Evolution** criteria, **Quality** range criteria, and **Cost** range criteria.

INVENTION/EVOLUTION CRITERIA (I/E CRITERIA)

The invention criterion is the reason why a product or service came into existence in the first place. It identifies which basic human desire it satisfies. The evolution criterion, on the other hand, shows how this product or service evolves into the future, satisfying additional human desires. For example, the invention criterion of the pen is to produce a written document for preservation or "to write to preserve" for short. One of its evolution criterion is to be able to write continuously without dipping for ink [seen in older models] or "to facilitate continuous writing" in short. The other evolution criteria are – better grip, smoother writing, color ink options and so on. The invention criteria and the evolution criteria together make up the utility value of the product or service.

The invention criterion of a product or service never changes in its lifetime. If it changes, it becomes another product altogether. For example, if we want to write and erase at the same time to modify the original writing, then it becomes a pencil. The basic invention criterion of a pencil is different from a pen. If a pencil writes very legibly but is hard to erase, it will fail in the marketplace. In the same manner, if the writing of a pen is erasable, then it will fail too. A product or service will have only one invention criterion. However, it may have several evolution criteria to satisfy more human desires. For example, the invention criterion of an automobile is "to transport" and its evolution criteria are "interior comfort," "music system," "higher speed," and so on. Early cars were very crude and only satisfied the invention criterion "to transport." They were not comfortable, and certainly did not have ABS or air bags. These primitive cars evolved gradually into modern cars to satisfy growing human desires. Remember, the invention criterion never changed in these cars, if it does, it will become another product.

When a product/service establishes in the market, it will undergo gradual evolution to satisfy more human desires. For example, if we desire a faster car, then "speed" becomes the evolutionary criteria and brings sports cars to the market, driving the technology behind a high-speed engine. Similarly, if we desire good music in the car, then a "music system" becomes the evolutionary criteria that will drive the radio, CD player, and speaker products to evolve. If, for some reason, the majority of people did not want to listen to music while driving, then these automotive music products would not have appeared in the market in the first place. Now, after being in the market, each one of these products will undergo several upgrades as, and when, technology improves.

To make the concept clearer, let us take two examples. Firstly, let us take the example of a coffee maker, see how it evolved and will continue to evolve into the future. The invention criterion of a coffee maker was, and is, to satisfy our desire for a cup of "fresh brewed coffee." As time went by and we got busier, the evolution criteria, "time saving" features influenced its future evolution. We wanted to make good coffee, but quickly. In older models, we had to heat water and pour it into the filter. Now, the machine heats the water itself, saving time.

Next, coffee makers attached to a water supply, eliminating the requirement to pour water, saving more time. Expect time saving features to dominate future modifications. Though there are many aesthetically designed coffee makers, if either of these two criteria – fresh brewed coffee or time saving – is compromised, they will fail in the market.

The next time you see a new coffee maker, notice its design criteria. If it is just shape, color, or some other irrelevant feature like an embedded digital clock or an alarm setting, and if it is slow in making coffee, it will not be in the market for a long time. It all comes down to how quickly the coffee is brewed– and how little human interaction is required.

What is the future of coffee makers? Already there are programmable designs allowing preparation of the coffee in the morning before you wake. In the future, there will be coffee makers with embedded computer chips, which understand our habits and prepare the coffee in advance with no programming needed. They will collect data on how often we made coffee and at what times, for a week or two, and then start mimicking our usage. Coffee makers will continue to evolve saving us more time and understand our habits to satisfy our desires to greater extent.

The future of any home device, not just coffee makers, is moving toward becoming interactive, with an understanding of our usage patterns, not just to save us time, but being proactive in their service.

Now, let us take the example of a "restaurant," see how it evolved and will continue to evolve into the future.

Traditionally, the invention criterion of a restaurant has always been to serve "tasty food." Over centuries, this desire has created innumerable recipes. This primary criterion will not change and humans will continue to be innovative to satisfy their taste buds.

However, as economic activity increased in cities, an evolution criterion, "food availability," began to influence restaurants. This evolution criterion has led to the mushrooming of restaurants all around us. Now restaurants fill cities.

Further, as time progressed, another evolution criterion –, "time to spend," – began to influence the technological evolution of restaurants. This gave rise to two types of restaurants: full service restaurants for people who want to spend more time and fast food restaurants for people who do not have time to spend.

The first kind of restaurant is for people who want to meet for business discussions, family gatherings or holiday parties. The second kind of restaurant is for busy working people or travelers.

Let us see how these two types of restaurants evolved from past to present, and their future. For the first type, where people want to spend more time, restaurant interior ambiance became the focal point. Our desire for a cozy environment has brought in various types of interior designs and is evolving still.

For the second type of restaurant, speed is of the essence. People want to pick up food and leave instead of dining in. Many restaurants offer drive-thru facilities to address this time criterion.

Now let us use the principle of desire to look into the future of these restaurants. In both types of restaurants, to satisfy the "food availability" criterion, there will be a clustering of restaurants, similar to mini-food courts, to give customers more choices in one place rather than in several individual restaurants. This food-cluster will resemble a regular restaurant, but one person will take orders for **multiple cuisines**. These food clusters answer one nagging problem in today's world – cuisine options. During family gatherings, each of us has our own preference in cuisine, but we all end up in one restaurant that caters only to some of us because the availability of multiple cuisines in any one place is lacking. Even fast food restaurants will be one-stop fast food clusters, where one order includes several cuisines to save even more time. These types of restaurants are already making their presence in some cities.

Looking further into the future, seated restaurants, to address the "interior ambiance" criterion, will offer multiple themes from which to choose in each of these clusters. The cluster will have individual areas where themes such as Chinese, Egyptian or Italian are offered. Going one step further into the future, clusters will use digital architecture rather than fixed decorations, where the theme of the restaurant will change each day, lending to a dynamic environment. Still farther into the future, customers will get to choose their own theme in individualized areas, choosing an ocean view or a mountain view. Even dining tables will become digital, offering world information right at the table. You could even work while eating.

In the case of fast food restaurants, apart from the clustering discussed above, more focus will be put on instant service to save us time. These fast food centers will become instantly faster in service. Whether we order food from our cell phone or local kiosk, the wait time will be next to zero. Instant service will become the future evolution criterion. To make this instant service a reality, restaurants will be automated, a concept which we are going to discuss later on.

The invention criteria in all of these restaurants will never change. Humans will continue to create new recipes and continue to invent better, faster cooking machines. From growing food to transportation to food preparation to the effect of food on our health, all will evolve together as one interrelated industry.

The above examples clearly indicate inventions and their technological evolutions follow human desires. Products and services continuously evolve to satisfy human desires even more. Though new inventions are an attempt to increase the living standard of the consumers, their continuous technological evolution requires an enormous amount of research. Research needs investment so businesses follow the ladder principle to increase the quality of products and services little by little to suit the end users' spending capacity. As human desires are never ending, technological evolution is perpetual.

QUALITY RANGE CRITERIA AND COST RANGE CRITERIA

The extent to which the quality of a product or service will evolve depends on how much we are willing to pay for it. Let us say, for example, a store is selling a box of toothpicks for 25¢ and another box of toothpicks – made of high-quality material – for $5. Most people will choose the cheaper one, as high quality in toothpicks is unnecessary as long as they are hygienic. Even if the second company has invested a lot of money in improving the quality of those toothpicks, for example, their texture, appearance, material used, and so on, it will still fail in the market or the market size will be very small, as quality and the cost are too high. For digital equipment, on the other hand, we would be willing to pay little more for higher quality, as quality is more important in those products.

The question then becomes, "How much quality do we need in a product or service?" or, "How much would a product or service evolve into the future?" This is where the "quality-ladder" appears. Each step of the ladder represents the quality-cost range, which is the buying capacity of the market. If there is a high quality but very expensive product that is well outside the range for the target market, that product/service will fail.

The diagram below shows the quality ladder.

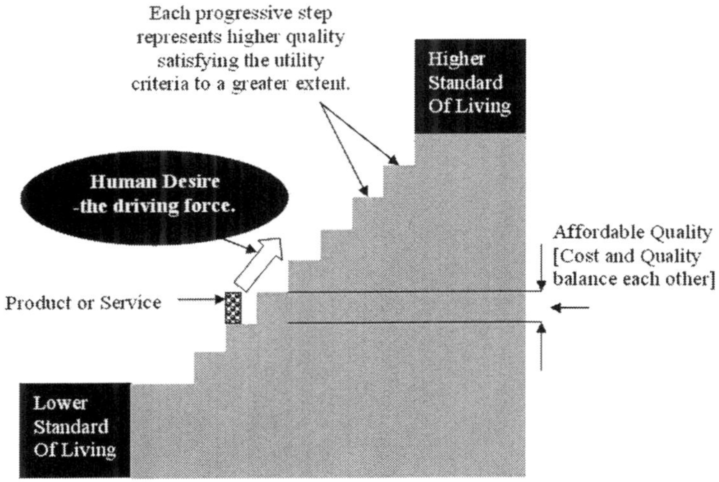

Fig-3: Quality Ladder

If you look at the above "quality ladder," you can see the quality of a product or service increases a step at a time to suit the buying capacity of the market. The quality and cost ultimately decide the fate of the product. The quality must be acceptable and the cost must be affordable to the targeted end user.

Every time a new version of a product releases into the market, it will have a little more quality than the previous one to suit the buying capacity of the market. This is the reason we see digital equipment (camera, cell phone, laptop, video game, etc.) that is better year after year, in steady, small increments. Many times cost will never change but quality and features will. Companies are reluctant to invest too much money in a product, making them more expensive when they have the potential to fail. The point being, quality and cost balance each other out, and the product evolves in increments.

Now lets use this quality-ladder concept in the evolution of restaurants that we discussed earlier. In restaurants, be it dine-in or fast food, our desire for higher quality and lower cost has brought about innovative appliances. We now see very sophisticated cooking machines in most restaurants. Compare this to utensils used hundred years ago. If you look at the history of any restaurant, you will see a pattern of quality improvement. Where there is more machine usage, the quality is high. Mass-produced items bring down costs and allow fast food restaurants to sell food for less. In restaurants, where customers dine in, the food is prepared to order with obviously higher costs.

Quality of cooking equipment will continue to improve following the ladder principle discussed earlier.

WE NEED TO MASTER THIS ART TO SEE THE FUTURE

Sometimes it is hard to identify the driving criteria, be it the invention or the evolution criteria. However, if we look at the history, we can easily trace the evolutionary path. We need not be great inventors to envision future of products and services. In fact, the focus of this book is not to teach how to invent things but to show the art of tracing the evolutionary path of products and services so we can grasp the forces driving this evolving world. It is an art we already possess. We only need to master it.

CHAPTER 5

THE PRINCIPLE OF GLOBALIZATION

THE MARKET SIZE

Although it is market demand that decides the fate of the inventions, market size decides how fast they will evolve. Larger-scale global markets bring more revenue to invest in research for further improvement in technology, rather than smaller, local markets.

Globalizing a product dramatically increases the pace of its technological evolution. We can easily see this impact in the world of digital gadgets. The demand for better laptops and better cell phones for example, is so high that millions of dollars are spent on improving them. This is possible because of huge revenue from the global market. Because the revenue is high, the competition is too. We see better digital cameras almost every year. Every new one is better than its predecessors. It is not just one modification; but continuous effort at the research table for engineers to improve them, to survive in this competitive world.

The diagram below shows the effect of market size on the evolutionary pace.

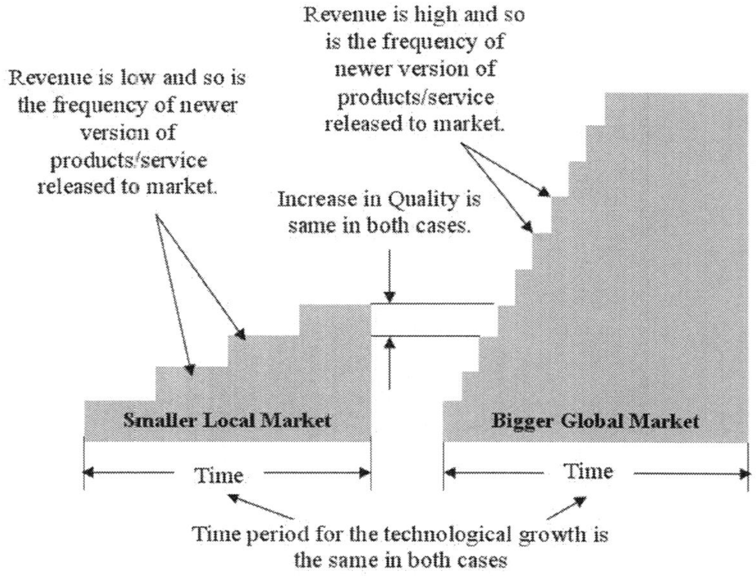

Fig 4: Effect of Market Size on Evolutionary Pace

This is the reason why consumers always look for brand products. They think larger companies do a better job in quality research and management, as they have higher revenue. Breaking into well-established markets is a big hurdle for new companies. They have no other option but to look for new innovative products that are not in the market yet. We have seen many instances of garage inventions developing into global businesses. The quest to innovate keeps innovators motivated to create new products, moving our technological evolution to higher levels.

WHAT EXACTLY IS GLOBALIZATION?

Globalization is not simply selling products globally. It is a continuous search for better skills (white collar jobs), better raw materials, better technology, low cost labor (blue collar jobs), and of course, bigger markets. Every one of these helps the companies remain competitive. A company may design a product in one country, manufacture it in another country, and sell it in an entirely different country.

For example, many luxury cruise ships are designed in countries wherever design skill is available and assembled in another country where low cost labor is available. They bring the best products from various countries around the world. Finally, it may be operated as a cruise line in the Caribbean where the market demand is high. Regardless of the complexity of such an arrangement, it is most efficient for the cruise line company to do business this way.

"Adaptive globalization" takes globalization a step further: countries export products that can adapt naturally to the target market so they become as effective as local products. For example, if a company making American pizza is globalized and then sold in Asia, it has to adapt to the local market to succeed. The obvious change is local flavor. When it adapts to the local market, suddenly it tastes very different. Likewise, a voice-activated GPS should understand the local language; movies must be dubbed to capture the interest of the local audience; the list of adaptive globalization is endless. To succeed, businesses have to adapt to target markets around the world.

Companies always compete to capture a bigger market share. To capture a bigger market, the cost has to be competitive. Typically, lower costs are achieved by mass production. Mass production can be done in two ways – using low cost labor or automation. As long as low cost labor is available around the world, "outsourcing" happens naturally to bring down the product/service cost.

OPENING THE FLOODGATE OF GLOBALIZATION

Globalization is not something new to the world. Trade is believed to have taken place throughout recorded human history. However, ancient trading was merely an exchange of food and other natural resources as there were no industrial products to trade. This is the reason ancient trades were on a small scale.

Noticeable international business activity occurred in the Industrial Age when products began to dominate the market. Unlike food and other natural resources, there is no limitation on consumption of products. In fact, consumption of products increases as the living standard increases. For instance, the daily consumption of food for a family does not vary much unless the family size itself increases. A similar constraint on the number of products consumed does not exist. Businesses that produce products also create jobs. Jobs bring more income to families. With higher income, people buy more goods and the economy grows.

During the era of industrialization, even though there were plenty of products to be traded, the pace of trade depended on communication. If we look at history and closely observe this path of globalization, we notice a predictable growth pattern. The growth of globalization was very closely associated with the growth of communication. As communication technology improved so did global trade.

Before computers, information flowed through communication media like telephone and printed media, as well as through business relations and personal contacts. Only established businesses were able to trade internationally and it was not an easy venture for new businesses.

After Information Technology evolved and computers came into existence, communication became much easier. It brought globalization to a new level. The newfound information media affected the life of ordinary people, too. We now can buy or sell anything online. Many people conduct business from home with the help of computers. Imagine selling a clock or an art painting a couple of decades ago to a customer in another country yourself. Today this is possible because of Information Technology.

If you look at the growth pattern of globalization, we notice it was actually the global information that was holding us back all these years from doing business with the rest of the world. Today there are billions of websites all over the world making the information flow possible. Information technology has finally opened the **"floodgate of globalization."**

LAND OF OPPORTUNITIES

Although human desire is the force behind the economic growth, how much people are willing to spend to increase their standard of living, determines the size of the market and thereby the pace of economic growth. Though all humans have desires, people in developed countries tend to spend more.

The very reason developed countries evolved so fast is because of their motivated market. The market is a great force when it comes to developing a country. The market gives rise to businesses and creates jobs. The market creates competition and increases the product quality. The market brings that needed professionalism in business. Ultimately, the market makes or breaks the economy in a country. When people are willing to spend more to improve their standard of living, a strong market emerges. This, in fact, is the main reason behind the success of developed countries.

People in developed countries spend more than people of underdeveloped ones spend – but not because they have more. It is not the dollar amount that is important, but the ratio of what people earn to what they spend. If you look at some slow developing countries, people save so much that their conservative habit slows the economic development in their own country. Although the banks are flooded with cash from savings, the businesses suffer because the market is not a spending market but a conservative one.

If an average family in one country spends a little more than another country, the economy in the first country grows a little faster than the second and over several decades this adds up significantly. We see a vast difference between a developed country and an underdeveloped country over time. It all comes down to how much people are willing spend to improve their standard of living from whatever they earn. This spending habit decides the pace of economic growth. A nation's economic status is in the hands of its own people.

Any country with a motivated market is a “land of opportunities.” Most developed countries are. New ideas, new inventions are highly appreciated in a motivated market. When people buy more, industries produce more.

GLOBALIZATION IS THE FASTEST WAY TO GROW

Although developed countries enjoy a higher standard of living, they face one hurdle for faster growth – ever escalating labor costs. When the standard of living increases, automatically the labor becomes expensive. This is true in all countries both developed and developing. A highly competitive market is always on the lookout for an answer, either low cost labor or automation.

As a complement to the above scenario, there is plenty of low cost labor available in underdeveloped countries. Some countries have low cost skilled labor as well. The standard of living in some countries is so low they can offer services for a fraction of what it costs in a developed country.

When we look at these two scenarios in the context of Information Technology opening the floodgate of globalization, it is not very surprising these countries found what they wanted. The exchange of labor force happened very seamlessly. However, no one had ever estimated the strength behind this global economy. The massiveness of globalization has surprised even the economic experts. Many question whether the world is going in the right direction.

While developed countries find low cost labor to produce goods and skilled labor to improve technology, the underdeveloped countries find great opportunities to grow their own economy. Many underdeveloped countries have transformed into developing countries.

When an underdeveloped country improves, we often ask, “What is there for us if another country improves?” or, “What good does it do our country if some other country’s standard of living goes up?” We fail to realize when the standard of living of one country improves, it becomes a customer in the global economy, increasing the global market size, thereby benefiting the rest of us.

Outsourcing appears to be one sided – moving jobs from developed countries to underdeveloped countries but in reality, it is a bi-directional transaction. For instance, many United States and European automobile companies are already selling cars in China, India, and other developing countries. These developing countries are a huge market for cell phone and other electronic gadgets as well. Many United States food chains operate franchises in these countries. Construction is booming, with most developing countries using American and European expertise, from architecture to design. Even the international tourism industry has improved as people in developing countries have more money now to spend on their vacation. More tourists are coming into developed countries to spend time and money. These developing countries have increased the size of the global market to such an extent the United States and European companies now have to produce more goods and services to satisfy this expanded market. You may call this reverse outsourcing.

However, the benefits of outsourcing will not come immediately. If jobs are outsourced now, it takes time for these underdeveloped countries to start contributing to the size of global market. When jobs are outsourced to developing countries, internal to that country several other supporting industries are created. These webs of industries bring up the standard of living of local people who in turn buy more products increasing the size of the global market. Further, more industries emerge to support this new demand. This positive feedback loop keeps expanding and makes the global economy stronger.

The United States and European countries are struggling to recover from the current economic slowdown because the current global market size is not big enough. Although developing countries like China and India are recovering at a faster pace, their market is not big enough to pull the United States and European economies up… yet. In the future as we begin to see more developing countries around the world, global economy would be much more powerful.

This power comes with underdeveloped countries developing faster. Underdeveloped countries grow faster only by globalization.

THE ILL EFFECTS OF RAPID GROWTH

Globalization does not come without problems. Economic growth in developing countries happens so rapidly these nations experience an economic jolt or boom. The scenario is entirely different in developed countries where industries evolved over several decades to improving their living standard steadily in all of their regions. There was enough time for overall economic growth.

On the other hand, developing countries are now flooded with industries and investments. Multinational companies have established billion dollar empires. Real estate values have grown exorbitantly high in a very short period because of a surge in real estate demand. Pre-existing poverty and newfound wealth do not go together very well. This is not steady growth like developed countries experienced; this rapid growth only occurs in some regions of the country. The rest of the regions are still very poor. The difference between rich and poor has caused unrest in society and administration as well. Corruption has shown its ugly face.

Globalization is a process of moving up the underdeveloped world. It is a very chaotic process. Though this problem will ease as poor citizen's standard of living steadily improves in these countries, it is a time consuming process if we let it progress on its own.

For instance, there is a great demand for low cost skilled labor in developed countries and the developing countries can supply it, as their population is large and waiting for opportunities. The problem, though, are "slow and expensive" education systems. It takes decades to open a school or a college in a remote, backward village. Even if schools and colleges open, the education path itself is very slow. By the time a student earns a college degree, he or she has spent years learning many irrelevant subjects. These countries must focus on "accelerated" and low-cost education rather than traditional paths, so their standard of living improves more quickly.

Replacing paper currency with electronic currency or digital money greatly reduces and eventually eliminates corruption and illegal transactions. Electronic currencies are very transparent and discourage people from breaking the law. However promising this concept looks, abolishing paper currency is not easy, as people still use it for daily transactions. Abolishing paper currency prematurely will only hurt the economy.

However, e-currency will naturally happen when globalization is well established. For businesses to conduct transactions faster, electronic currency becomes inevitable. Soon we will see devices like cell phones and other gadgets with transactional capability. Once these devices reach ordinary customers, then e-currency establishes itself inevitably. The end of paper currency era brings an end to many ills of the current age. How quickly this transformation happens depends on the pace of globalization.

HOW TO USE THIS PRINCIPLE TO SEE THE FUTURE

In a nutshell globalization is all about "involving more people to pull the weight." If a product or service seems expensive, consider if it has a global market. If not, consider what bottlenecks are keeping it from going global. Once we understand the bottlenecks, we will be able to find solutions. The best example is our healthcare system.

The size of the healthcare market, for instance, not only in the United States but also in many developed countries, is limited to their own population, thus making it very expensive. Technology is increasing the cost but revenue is limited. Many experts believe that making some policy changes will reduce the cost of healthcare. The truth is, we cannot stop technology from growing and every time technology grows, the healthcare cost increases that much. We need to identify the reason why it is not going global. Using the principle of globalization to identify bottlenecks in many industries where evolution of products or services slows is a great tool.

CHAPTER 6

THE PRINCIPLE OF AUTOMATION

GOING BEYOND HUMAN CAPABILITY

Automation comes to our lives inevitably as people desire higher efficiency beyond their capability. We are already seeing many instances of partial automation around us in ATM machines, self-checkout counters, airport e-check-in, and card scanning turnstiles on trains and buses, online banking, online shopping to name a few. We feel their evolutionary effect on our daily lives.

Before the invention of ATM machines, we literally had to wait for banks to open on business days to withdraw cash. ATM machines eliminate the bottleneck saving consumers a lot of time and enabling businesses to flourish. ATM machines are also becoming more interactive with customers.

Introducing ATM machines in towns and cities allow banks and businesses to make more transactions and move the economy faster. Just by eliminating the human element from one service, the whole business community gets a boost to move forward at a higher pace.

More than ATM machines, banks do business at a faster pace with credit cards and online banking, other examples of automation. The online banking business is so huge that if all online banking closed down forcing people to do their transactions in person, banks simply could not handle it. You may recall from history books, the amount of resistance people offered when computers were introduced in banks. Over the years this automation has created so many jobs and it has improved the pace of economy to such an extent that there is no going backwards from this level of automation unless we want to slow down our economy. This is just one illustration to show we are bringing automation into our lives because of our desire for higher efficiency, faster service and of course, lower cost.

Other types of automation have a positive impact on the pace of technological evolution, similar to ATMs.

IF AUTOMATION IS HELPING OUR ECONOMY, WHY ARE INDUSTRIES NOT FULLY AUTOMATED?

Many industries, such as bottling plants, packaging companies etc., have automated most of their jobs as they are continuous, 24/7, high-speed work. For jobs like heavy lifting, automation is the only answer. Car manufacturers have automated precision assemblies. The rest of the jobs are still manual.

We cannot completely automate our industries because robots and machines are still very expensive and manual labor is still relatively cheaper. A highly skilled labor force is required to research and develop the technology to build them. This makes the automated machines expensive. Can such an expensive automated machine replace a low-cost worker? It is highly unlikely until there is substantial demand for the products such automated machines produce. This is where globalization comes in.

THE EFFECT OF GLOBALIZATION ON AUTOMATION

Automation happens from a positive feedback loop of globalization. When globalization moves toward higher levels, we see high-paced economic activity and increased production rates. When industries find low cost labor, their production costs come down, increasing their market size both locally and globally. When their market size increases, their economic activity increases and they need bigger labor force both skilled and unskilled. This loop keeps expanding until most countries of the world are involved in the global economy, transforming them into fast developing countries.

This increased economic activity puts pressure on human efficiency. We already see people working harder to meet deadlines. This makes human labor gradually "less effective," forcing us towards automation. Here the term "less effective" should not be construed as "less efficient." It merely means that manual labor will reach its physiological limitation. As the labor cost becomes relatively expensive, it makes automation economically viable.

The only hurdle is the availability of technology. If the needed technology is available, businesses will move towards automation. When these three **"automation forces"** – **L**ess effective manual work, **E**xpensive labor and availability of **T**echnology (LET for short) – come together, automation happens seamlessly.

For instance, automatic scanning technology recently automated many toll roads, eliminating "less effective" manual labor. This saves travelers a considerable amount of time. After retraining, the same employees can sit at computers and manage this automated toll road system.

Online check-in is a good example of recent automation in the airline industry. Customers can now print their boarding passes well in advance, saving time at manual check-in counters. Fast checkout lanes are another good example of automation in supermarkets.

Wherever you see more economic activity, automation is showing up to replace less effective and expensive manual labor. Automation happens when manual labor is not able to keep up with the demand of the high-paced economic growth.

Automation will happen more rapidly in developed countries as labor is expensive and technology is readily available. Even the consumers in the developed countries expect faster services. Businesses always give way to these LET forces to remain competitive. Inventors rise to the challenge, creating alternative solutions to ease these LET forces. Ultimately it is the customers who reap the benefits of more efficient services.

Here is an illustration of why automation becomes inevitable in a huge global market. Let us say a company is supplying electric bulbs to a small local market using local laborers in a developed country. Over time, the business expands, becoming a global industry. As it begins catering to the global market, its production rate increases considerably. To meet high demand, the business has to hire more workers. Labor is expensive in most developed countries so outsourcing is inevitable to remain competitive. Outsourcing brings prices further down, increasing the market size both locally and globally. This expanded market leads to even more labor outsourcing. Despite extensive outsourcing, the production rate reaches its limit as manual labor is less effective. Huge labor force requirement to meet this growing global demand will eventually become a bottleneck, and also increases the labor cost. Even the competing businesses will be facing similar shortcomings.

Now, let us say this company adapts full or partial automation in their production system. It begins to capture a much larger market share, because it can now produce at a **higher speed**. The quality will be "consistent machine quality" – because of automation. Increased production rates mean speedier deliveries, winning the industrial production race against other competitors. This higher market share quickly compensates for the large investments made in the automation. Remember: automation in any industry is very cost sensitive; it will not happen unless the market demand is huge. Only an extensive globalization can cause automation to show up.

In the above scenario, it appears automation becomes inevitable in all global businesses when the global economy expands. The massive outsourcing that is happening today is a step towards automation. The automation pace may not be the same in all countries. As discussed earlier, the intensity of the three LET factors – Less effective manual work, Expensive labor and Technology – decide the pace of automation. This means there will be more automation in developed countries, less in developing countries and little to none in underdeveloped countries.

However, as the underdeveloped counties develop, they all will go thru the same stages of globalization and automation.

LEVELS OF AUTOMATION

Automation happens in stages or levels. For example, the ATM machine is a fully automated product by itself. For our discussion, let's consider it level-1 automation as people can interact with that machine to get services without any human intervention.

What do you think the next level of automation in this machine should be? Do you feel these dumb machines should be more intelligent to understand our needs? Will another layer of automation that understands our needs and tells the machine what to do be desirable?

In the future, there will be another layer on top of existing ATM machines with level-2 capability, which recognizes you through facial recognition, fingerprint, or another technology. As you approach the machine, it customizes the screen to match your habits and continues to learn about you every time you use the machine. For instance, if you are in the habit of withdrawing $100 every Friday, the cash button will appear on the main screen for you to press to get your usual $100 if you visit an ATM on a Friday. You will not waste any time going through the screen menu; instead, you quickly get the cash and move on. This level-2 system constantly collects customer data and directs the level-1 ATM machine on interactions with customers. It understands your financial status, pending payments, commitments and so on and may even prompt you on the screen for payments that are pending.

In the future, when level-2 automation enters the market, all you need do is go near an ATM machine and it will guide you much like your personal manager.

Level-3 automation evolves a step further. This level will constantly analyze the data and provide advice on future enhancements to the system itself. It interacts with the ATM manufacturing plant and helps to build a better machine each time it is upgraded. Level-3 will collect data from "interaction activity" between the customer and the machine, analyze it and decide how fast it has to evolve to serve better. This will be like automated evolution, bringing higher levels of automation more rapidly.

The other noticeable change that may happen to ATM machines is, once currency becomes electronic, ATM machines, as cash dispensers, may become obsolete as the invention criterion changes. However, the same machines then may become bank kiosks or personal financial centers depending on the requirement at that time.

In the current world, ATM machines are manually assembled, even though they are level-1. The company that assembles them is still in level-0. If you consider the finance industry as a whole, ATM machines represent only partial automation. With more globalization, the cost of ATM machines will decrease, further increasing the size of the market. This positive feedback loop initiates automation in the assembly of ATM machines as well. As we move up in the globalization ladder, automation establishes in all industrial sectors.

DO WE REALLY NEED AUTOMATION?

Automation is the only answer to manmade disasters. We have witnessed bridges collapsing, aircrafts crashing, and the recent tragic offshore oil leak. With thousands of bridges, why have only a few collapsed? When we have built and used many aircrafts, why have only a few crashed?

In the case of bridges, for instance, engineers may have unintentionally overlooked some parameters; maybe a wrong material, maybe more load than expected or simply poor design or maintenance. If machines fabricate and manage bridges instead of humans, there will be more consistency and fewer errors. If there is a mishap, it is easy to identify the problem and correct it in the next enhancement. The same argument goes with every other man made disaster.

Even at level-1 automation, human errors will carry into the automation to end up as disasters. This is where level-2 automation comes in, eliminating human error and making the system more reliable. At level-3 automation, as explained above, the machines learn about themselves and evolve.

Unfortunately, we have not yet reached level-1, in either bridge construction or in building aircraft. Offshore drilling is only partially automated. Disasters can be easily averted when higher levels of automation are reached. In most places today, humans are handling level-1, level-2, level-3 and all other possible levels manually. This is the reason we are not able to predict or manage disasters when they happen.

To achieve higher levels of safety, we need to move into higher levels of automation. This will happen only from massive globalization. The diagram below shows various phases of automation.

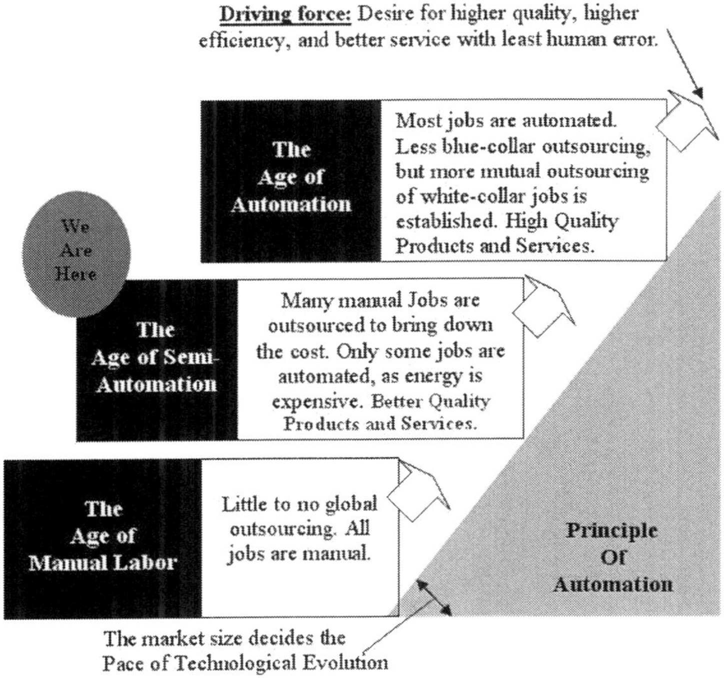

Fig 5: Phases of Automation

EFFECTS OF AUTOMATION ON OUR OWN LIVES

What can we expect when machines are doing our work? We will see considerable job losses during the early stages of automation and equally massive job creations in new areas. We are already seeing such overlaps. It is not uncommon to see job openings that were not there before. Companies providing "search engine" services or "online stores" a few decades ago were unfamiliar. Today those companies employ thousands of people all over the world. Looking at job losses from an evolutionary angle requires we look at both sides of the coin. We are losing jobs in some areas where manual labor is less effective yet creating jobs where automation is needed.

There is no one-to-one relation between job losses and new job creation. However, automation always causes more economic activity as we saw with the ATM machines. With automation prices come down and service level goes up creating the positive feedback loop of globalization. When economic activity increases, job opportunities increase in many industrial sectors.

To understand automation and the resultant job losses, look at the overall economic development rather than any one particular company where jobs are lost. For instance, if highway tollbooths lay off people, another company that manages these automatic systems or supporting businesses will be hiring employees. Again, here we should not look at one-to-one relation. These companies in turn will be supporting many other companies, such as computer networks for faster connectivity, hardware suppliers, and a host of other new infrastructure needed to support the business. Similarly, if fast checkout counters lay off people, the company that designs and programs these machines and all supporting businesses will be hiring employees.

Many lost jobs may not come back as the steps towards globalization and automation are irreversible. Our job market is changing so fast that a person who loses his/her job may not be able to find a similar job available. Instead, they need to look for industries that are creating new jobs. If knowledge or training in Information Technology is lacking, then retraining is required.

Here is another illustration of the effect of automation on our jobs. The furniture in our homes, for instance, used to be handmade. Carpenters cut the wood, prepared the surface, and assembled the final product by hand. Now, high precision computer-controlled machines cut and prepare the wood with humans only handling the final assembly. This is the reason modern furniture is becoming less and less expensive as technology has improved. Compare a wooden chair that costs only $10, to one manually built by a skilled carpenter, paid $50 or more an hour. How many chairs must that person make in an hour for the company to make a profit? That business cannot survive without automation. Carpentry skills are not needed for mass production purposes. The skill needed is the ability to manage machines.

This does not mean there are no carpentry jobs any more. Today, carpenters are focusing on customized work, which is not mass-produced, like home building, making custom cabinets and furniture and so on. Even in these jobs, they are faced with automation. They have to use the latest fast machines to do the job quickly and more precisely resulting in high quality work in less time. Machines already prepare most of the wood used with less human labor wasted. This is just one example to show the effect of automation on our jobs and careers. If you closely look at the history of any profession, you will see a pattern of continuous automation.

In this fast changing world, someone who loses a blue-collar job and finds it difficult to find a similar job must realize that **the world has moved on** and those jobs are not there around anymore. They should seize an opportunity to change careers.

Process by process, job-by-job, automation is creeping into our lives, improving our lifestyle. This automation blends so seamlessly into our lives people many times do not notice it. For instance, have you ever wondered how people heated their lunch before the microwave oven? Surely, if your microwave oven breaks down, you will find ways to work around it. However, it is so inconvenient and microwave oven is so affordable, a new one will quickly replace the broken one. The same argument goes for every home appliance we have today. This is the reason why automation is irreversible. It is blended into our lives, making our lives richer and many times gives us no other option. Life has become very hectic and stressful, making the need for these technological products even more necessary, with less and less time to perform such functions ourselves.

Eventually automation will have profound effect on everyone's career. If we are unprepared for this future shock, it will have a negative impact on our technological evolution, as people misinterpret the changing world. Many people have questioned the ethics behind automation when it is going to cause extensive job losses.

Here is an illustration that answers such a question. Suppose there are two companies, selling the same product for the same price including shipping and handling. Company A delivers the product in **two** business days, while company B delivers it in **five** business days. Which one will customers prefer? Company A is fully automated and the machines do most of the job, whereas Company B is not automated yet and human laborers handle all the work. Non-automated companies cannot compete with automated ones. Unknowingly, the world votes with its pocketbook and is moving toward automation.

The reality is, during the Age of Automation, most businesses face an ultimatum of "automate or give up." They simply cannot go back in time to manual labor. If they do, they lose out to competition, as manual labor cannot produce goods at machine speed. Speed and quality will be the winner and will become one of the major evolutionary criteria in all the industries.

HOW DO WE LOOK AT THE FUTURE USING THIS PRINCIPLE?

The Age of Automation will not only be fascinating but also gives us the needed support to lead a safe and comfortable life. This is the age we will feel safe from global disasters, having a layer of machines to do the tedious tasks. There will be fewer catastrophes because of human error. Sophisticated machines will predict future catastrophes more accurately. It is everyone's dream to reach that level. As our technological advancement is unstoppable, eventually we all will reach this point, but the question is when? How do we make this happen quicker?

One of the fastest ways to bring automation into our industries is by increasing the pace of the globalization. As discussed earlier, the cost of products and services depends on three resources – Raw material (**R**), Energy (**E**), and Labor (**L**). The cost of energy is the most critical among these. If energy costs decrease, the cost of raw materials decreases, too, as we use energy to extract raw materials. This brings the cost of products down substantially, moving globalization to higher levels, leading to eventual automation.

The most practical way to produce cheap energy is by automating its production such as through the evolutionary robot-assisted-production (**RAP**) method that will be discussed in coming chapters.

On the other hand, if we fail to make any effort to address "throughput" of energy production now, the global economy will reach the energy bottleneck sooner rather than later and experience frequent recessions. We already see the effects of rising energy prices and its effect on economic growth. Automating energy production eases the future energy crisis and also accelerates the process of reaching the Age of Automation.

CHAPTER 7

THE PRINCIPLE OF TECHNOLOGICAL EVOLUTION

THE TWO PLAYMATES

When people spend money to increase their living standard, they not only grow the economy but also drive technological evolution. Here is the distinction between economic growth and technological evolution. A car company expanding to produce more cars is considered economic growth. If the same car company manufactures cars that are more efficient, it is technological growth. When we buy a car, we promote the economy; however, when we shop for a more efficient car, we promote better technology.

The economic growth drives the technological growth and vice versa – and our desires drive both. Without human desire, there is neither economic growth nor technological growth.

Which is more important: sophisticated technology or strong economy? The truth is, one can't be better without the other. Suppose, for instance, engineers design gigantic tidal barriers to protect coastal cities from hurricanes caused by global warming. Will we have the financial capability to build such mega structures? Only an equally strong economy could handle it. If our economy is weak, all our technological marvels will remain on the drawing board.

To understand the principle of technological evolution, we need to understand the implicit relation between "globalization" and "automation." Globalization increases the economic activity of the world, creating a need for automation. Automation on the other hand, makes it easy for the globalization to happen.

For instance, washing clothes is a manual service and difficult to globalize. As technology grew, businesses developed washing machines, which quickly became a global product and is now sold in every big box store. This local service was globalized because of automation. Further, the same globalization brings in more automation to produce more machines.

Same argument goes with dish washing machines, microwaves, toasters, and a host of friendly machines around us.

When a process is automated it becomes a global product, in short, automation helps in globalization.

Without automation, globalization will be exceedingly slow. In the past, we grew at a very slow pace, with slow transportation and slow communications. The telex and telegram systems we had in the past are all examples of early stages of automation that were very slow. Now, with faster communication networks, our globalization speed has picked up. We cannot imagine outsourcing so many jobs without these faster networks. The pace of automation decides the pace of globalization.

These two human endeavors, globalization and automation, together drive our technological evolution and make our global economy stronger. One cannot succeed without the other. It resembles a seesaw, where a single child cannot play alone.

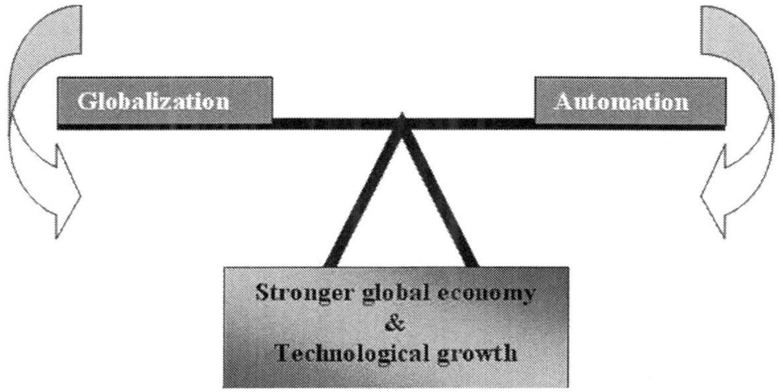

Fig 6: Globalization and Automation – the two playmates

While globalization represents the quantitative aspect of economy, automation represents the qualitative aspect of economy. Both quantity and quality matters for the technological evolution. If we build a huge bridge using manual labor, we only help build the economy. However, if we build the same bridge, with sophisticated tools and machines, we progress technologically.

Another analogy is that if we can represent automation as a two-dimensional face, then its depth represents globalization. This three dimensional model of automation and globalization totally represents the technological evolution.

TECHNOLOGICAL MARVELS

You may have read about or seen TV programs on world history about fascinating inventions from old civilizations, trying to achieve more than what they could. Researchers have been unearthing intriguing inventions like gears, clocks, even computers and airplanes dating back several thousand years and have wondered how someone from an ancient civilization could have built them. If we understand the principles of technological evolution, there is nothing to be surprised about such inventions. All civilizations have inventors, designing and dreaming about the future. Just as we dream about our future, our ancestors dreamed of their future, which is our present. Did they ever succeed building those machines in their time? Possibly as experimental devices but not as real products; they were lacking an advanced economy to support such advanced technology. A great invention needs an equally powerful economy.

If the economy remains healthy, then technological advancements happen continuously. If, on the other hand, the economy is weak, no matter how grand our ideas and how deep our desires are, they will be just dreams.

The surprising fact in all these evolutionary phases is, "Survival from extinction level threats" will never become the driving force. The driving force will always be our desire for better living.

Comfort and luxury will remain the driving forces for future technological evolution. Our desire for better living makes us **"technologically stronger"** day-by-day and eventually capable of surviving extinction level threats.

As we enter the Age of Automation, we will become stronger and more capable of surviving global disasters. Our technological evolution will move us at a faster pace going forward, as machines do most of the jobs. Further on, we will slowly emerge out of our current eco-dependency and into an eco-free Space Age, much more advanced than the earthly life and strong enough to survive any celestial threats. This book is all about walking this evolutionary path toward our inevitable destiny.

CHAPTER 8

THE PRINCIPLE OF ECONOMIC RECESSION

THE NEGATIVE FEEDBACK LOOP

Humans have two good qualities: the "desire to spend" and the "desire to conserve." While both may seem at odds with one another, in fact they are two sides of the same coin. When people spend, the economy grows, and when they conserve, the economy slows down. The reason people spend and the reason they conserve decides the fate of the economy.

People become conservative and buy/invest less for various reasons. Losing money in the stock market and real estate market are well-known reasons for people to become conservative. When people spend less or postpone their normal spending, it affects the real economy, as our industries and economy in general are highly dependent on our spending. When spending slows, industries produce less and may lay off people. Small businesses that cannot absorb this slowdown declare bankruptcy. Once the economy slows down, even regular consumers become more conservative in their spending. This negative feedback loop is a self-destructive force, which eventually brings our economy to a halt. **Recession is the result of the "negative feedback loop" of an economic slowdown.** This is why governments spend billions of dollars to stimulate the economy to break this negative feedback loop.

ECONOMY CAN HURT ITSELF

The concept of "credit" was developed to grow the economy faster and reduce the bottleneck of cash availability. Though credit has a very positive impact on our economy, it has a huge negative impact when not regulated. The unregulated easy credit creates fictitious growth of the economy exposing both producers and consumers to a higher risk.

During high economic growth, easy credit motivates people to buy or invest more, be it a car or real estate or any product of value. There is nothing wrong in using credit; however, if people use credit to buy beyond what they can afford to pay back, they end up creating a fictitious economic world. **This means companies produced more goods than they were supposed to produce.**

Here is an example to understand the impact of easy credit on our economy. Suppose one million people each spend a thousand dollars shopping in a year, using their own available credit. This amounts to one billion dollars flowing in the economy. Companies produced goods and services to meet this demand. It is also possible some new companies entered the market to meet this demand. Now, let us say the one million people have reached their credit limit. Some responsible customers paid back their loans and continued to use their credit cards, while others who were not capable of repaying their credit card balance, began to use other credit cards, risking themselves and the economy even further. These risky customers had no means to repay their debts. When these risky customers fail to repay and then declare bankruptcy, it not only hurts creditors but also hurts companies who produced the goods and have planned more for the growing economy. They may have hired more people and bought more inventories for future growth. Adding to this confusion, many new industries were established assuming the economy was growing fast.

In the real world, these numbers could be bigger; instead of one million there could be ten million or more risky customers involved in this reckless spending – even more globally. In addition, the spending amount could be as much as $10,000, $20,000, or more per person. This amounts to hundreds of billions of fictitious dollars floating in the economy.

Now, when these risky customers after reaching their credit limit are unable to payback their loans and are no longer part of the potential market, companies will suddenly experience slower sales and their profits plummet. The money they will have invested to produce more products is now at stake. Eventually they start laying off employees, which will have ripple effect on the other industries. This is the beginning of the **"negative feedback loop."** These risky customers may not cause a recession however, may initiate the economic slow down. Once this loop forms, it continues to slow the economy. Credit, which facilitates fast economic growth, could be devastating if not regulated.

The same easy credit causes bubbles in the real estate markets too. Remember, real estate value depends purely on demand. If fictitious demands stemming from easy credit drive up the market, bubbles are bound to happen.

Though this is how our economy works, the easy credit devil is right behind the economic boom to bite it if not regulated. While regulatory agencies are blamed for this, their failure to regulate is attributed to their inability to decide how much to regulate and when to regulate. The volume of financial data in the financial world is growing at an astonishing speed and it is difficult to handle it without well-developed software. Until our Information Technology catches up to the needs of our fast changing world, regulation is not an easy task.

Information Technology is our "Window" to the financial world; Information Technology has catapulted our economy to this level and only it can control its growth. The higher its sophistication (clarity), the better our view of the financial world will be. It is not that recessions will happen only in the current age and will be totally absent in the Age of Automation. Recession happens every time Information Technology lags behind the changing world. It does not matter at what evolutionary phase we are. A closely monitored economy is the fastest way to progress.

From an evolutionary point of view, every recession keeps us technologically weaker. When our technological evolution pauses, every day we are losing the opportunity to move closer to the Age of Automation.

CHAPTER 9

THE BOTTLENECKS

The five principles of technological evolution will form the foundation that will help us develop the Art of Looking into the Future.

Principle of Globalization

Principle of Economic Recession

Principle of Automation

Principle of Human Desire

Principle of Technological Evolution

When we use these five principles (or G-R-A-D-E principles for short) to look into the future of our world, we see various bottlenecks that obscure this view. When we look at these problems from an evolutionary angle, they naturally shape themselves into solutions. The diagram below shows the positive feedback loop of globalization and the bottlenecks for its growth.

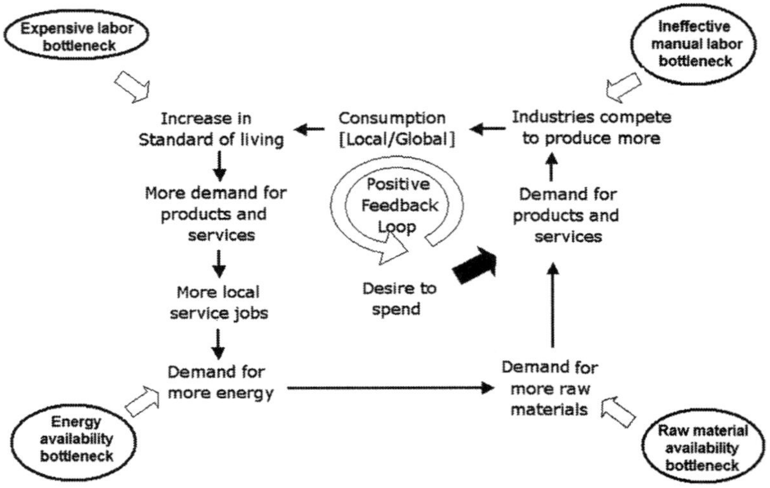

Fig 7: Positive Feedback Loop of Globalization

Part III of the book is all about looking at the above bottlenecks from an evolutionary angle. Using these five G-R-A-D-E principles, we will find evolutionary solutions not only to these bottlenecks but also to various other world problems.

Part IV of the book takes us a little further into the future where we explore the inevitable Age of Automation, its future comforts, and its inevitable consequences. This will give us a feel of how strong humankind could become, to face future extinction level threats.

Part V of the book is all about survival from global warming. We will explore how our technological evolution could outpace global warming, in order to survive.

PART III

In Search of Solutions

IN THIS PART:

CHAPTER 10

EVOLUTIONARY SOLUTION TO THE HEALTHCARE CRISIS

THE CRISIS

In order to adapt and evolve we must remain healthy as individuals and as a species. Unfortunately, the current state of our healthcare is in peril, as costs increase every year.

According to the United States Department of Health and Human Services, national healthcare expenditures grew 6.1 percent to $2.2 trillion in 2007, or $7,421 per person, and accounted for 16.2 percent of the Gross Domestic Product.

In 1970, total healthcare spending was about $75 billion, or only $356 per person. In less than 40 years, these costs have grown to $2.2 trillion, or $7,421 per person.

It is not only in the United States that costs are increasing, but also in every developed and developing country. However, the rise in healthcare costs in the United States far exceeds that of other countries.

The chart below shows the Healthcare Spending in U.S since 1965.

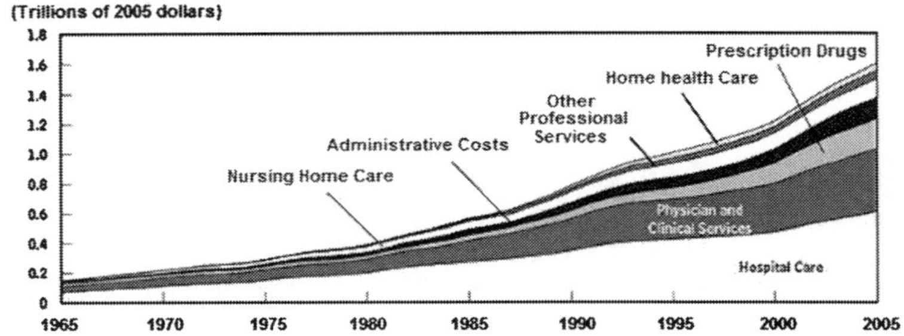

Fig 8: Real Spending on Health Care in Selected Categories, 1965 to 2005

Source: Congressional Budget Office based on data on spending on health services and supplies, as defined in the national health expenditure accounts, maintained by the Centers for Medicare and Medicaid Services. Note: Spending amounts are adjusted for inflation using the gross domestic product implicit price deflator from the Bureau of Economic Analysis

The experts' explanation of rapidly increasing healthcare costs is people are getting more care, much of which is associated with new medical technologies. Some analysts say the availability of more expensive, state-of-the-art drugs and technological services fuels healthcare spending. Not only is this because the development costs of these products must be recouped by the industry, but also because they are generating consumer demand for more intense, costly services, even if they are not necessarily cost effective.

Who is receiving these state-of-the-art diagnoses and treatments? The nature of healthcare in the United States has changed dramatically over the past century, with longer life spans and better care for people with chronic diseases.

The data below shows an increase in the usage of some of the latest technologies over time in the United States

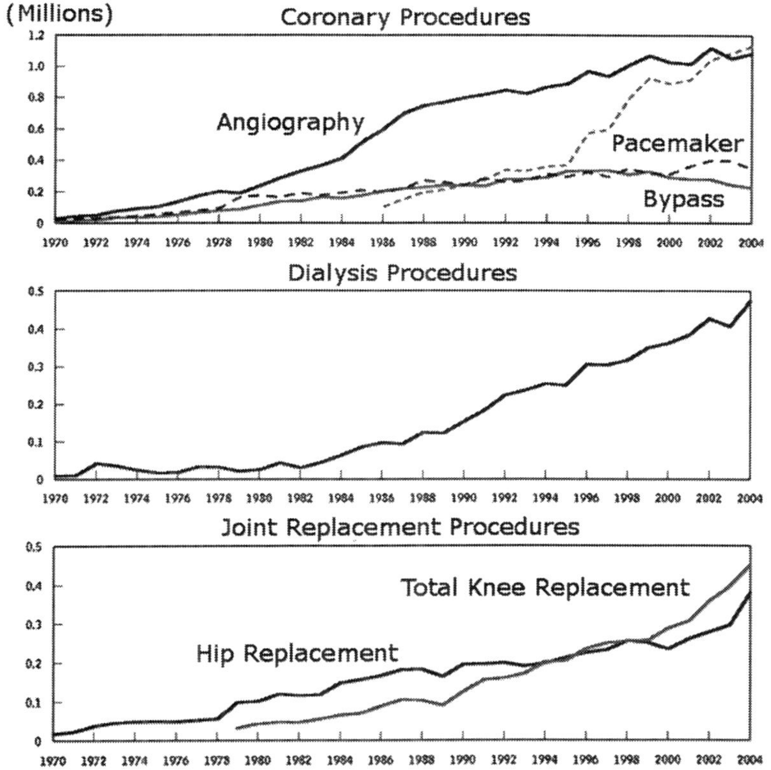

Fig 9: Use of Selected Health Care Procedures by People Aged 50 or Older, 1970 to 2004

Source: "Technological Change and the Growth of Health Care Spending." A CBO Paper - January 2008. U.S. Congress – Congressional Budget Office based on data from the National Center for Health Statistics.

It is estimated healthcare costs for chronic disease treatment accounts for over 75 percent of national healthcare expenditures. According to the Centers for Disease Control and Prevention, chronic diseases are the leading causes of death and disability in the United States. Healthcare technology advances every year. Advanced medical technology diagnoses more and more people with new problems every day, increasing the number of patients receiving treatment.

As recently as a few decades ago, diagnosing cancer was relatively rare. Now, doctors diagnose many types of cancers on a regular basis. Many argue that modern habits cause cancer in more people. Though true to some extent, the reality is, we simply did not have the tools or technology to diagnose it as easily in the past. Once diagnosed these diseases have to be treated.

Clinical developments continue to increase the longevity and improve the quality of life of many Americans – gene therapy for cancer treatment, less invasive surgical techniques, advances in reproductive technology, infection control, and so on. All these new technologies add to the cost of healthcare.

This sophisticated medical technology results in expensive treatments and is a major cause of higher healthcare costs today. ***There is a direct relation between the technological developments and healthcare costs.***

Health insurance premiums continue to grow as healthcare cost keeps climbing. Many people argue private insurance companies are the cause of these higher costs of healthcare. However, to some extent, they are responsible for the higher costs because of their own inherent overhead management costs, even after making these insurance companies more efficient (which is going to happen eventually), increasing costs will not go away until the root cause of the problem – **Technology** – is addressed.

SHOULD DOCTORS ORDER FEWER TESTS TO BRING DOWN THE COST? THE ANSWER IS NO.

The current trend among many physicians is to order as many tests as presumably relevant, and this surely increases healthcare costs. The reason for ordering more tests is twofold. One is protection from malpractice lawsuits, and the other is to serve as many patients as possible in their limited clinic hours while making more accurate diagnoses.

Many healthcare professionals argue that doctors could understand illnesses better by spending more time with patients. That would help them order tests that were genuinely needed and eliminate unnecessary ones.

More tests may seem unnecessary, but will help in making an accurate diagnosis and many times will unearth some hidden problems the patient never even knew about. Many tumors and other diseases may not show any symptoms until they become life threatening. Many times these conditions are discovered while investigating some other health problem. More tests are always life saving.

THE EVOLUTIONARY SOLUTION

To understand the rising cost of healthcare and eventually to find a solution, let us use the principle of globalization. Just like any other industry, if a product were mass-produced or if a service were mass supplied, the cost will decrease. As we have learnt, globalization is all about "involving more people to pull the weight." In the United States alone, we are spending trillions of dollars on healthcare, but our market size is limited to our population. Although some healthcare companies are exporting medicine and healthcare equipment, they still have a long way to go. Without globalization, the collected revenue of the healthcare market will be limited.

In a similar fashion, computers were very expensive when the market was small, but became very affordable despite its technological sophistication with a global market. It is merely a numbers game – the bigger the market the cheaper the product. Increasing the market size will substantially reduce healthcare costs.

SIZE OF GLOBAL HEALTHCARE MARKET

World population has exceeded 6.5 billion and is growing. Everyone needs healthcare. There is a huge demand for physicians throughout the world. The availability of good healthcare varies from country to country and from region to region. The data from the World Health

Organization (WHO) indicates that in the African region, there are only 2.3 physicians per 1,000 people, compared with 24.8 per 1,000 in the American regions.

	Total health workforce		Health service providers		Health management and support workers	
WHO region	Number	Density (per 1000 population)	Number	Percentage of total health workforce	Number	Percentage of total health workforce
Africa	1 640 000	2.3	1 360 000	83	280 000	17
Eastern Mediterranean	2 100 000	4.0	1 580 000	75	520 000	25
South-East Asia	7 040 000	4.3	4 730 000	67	2 300 000	33
Western Pacific	10 070 000	5.8	7 810 000	78	2 260 000	23
Europe	16 630 000	18.9	11 540 000	69	5 090 000	31
Americas	21 740 000	24.8	12 460 000	57	9 280 000	43
World	59 220 000	9.3	39 470 000	67	19 750 000	33

Fig 10: Global health workforce, by density

Note: All data for latest available year. For countries where data on the number of health management and support workers were not available, estimates have been made based on regional averages for countries with complete data.

Data source: World Health Organization. Global Atlas of the Health Workforce (http://www.who.int/globalatlas/default.asp).

The majority of the world population is poor. The actual size of the global healthcare market depends on the cost of the healthcare. If the cost is high, only a few can afford it; however, if the cost is low, a significant population can afford good healthcare. Cost and market size always work against each other. Most products and services start with high cost and gradually become cheaper as the market grows. If the healthcare market goes global, it will be no different.

GLOBALIZING HEALTHCARE

Medical diagnosis has two components to it. One is a consultation service where a physician interacts with patients for diagnosis and the other is a product which includes diagnostic tools like CAT scans, MRI machines, and so on, that gives more information about the ailment. The first is a service while the second is a product.

Globalizing the consultation service increases revenue and increases the demand for the diagnostic tools. Globally mass producing the diagnostic tools make them affordable. The more tests doctors order, the more demand exists for the diagnostic tools. Although this sounds simple, how do we practically globalize healthcare? The following sections describe some new innovative concepts which will help in globalization.

GLOBALIZATION OF THE CONSULTATION SERVICE (CONCEPT OF MRM)

The initial consultation with a doctor is the gateway to our healthcare system. This physician consultation service can be globalized by developing a futuristic Medical Record Mapping (MRM) technology. This hypothetical (for now) software diagnoses patients from the comfort of their homes.

Anyone with a health problem logs into the MRM system and submits their symptoms. The MRM sends this information to several doctors or hospitals to compare with their patient's electronic medical records. For simplicity we can consider this mapping as just matching of records, although a record-mapping algorithm could be quite complex, beyond the scope of this discussion.

If there are too many matches, then the software recommends additional tests based on criteria set by those doctors or hospitals. Once the patient has those tests, the MRM tries again to narrow down to some good diagnostic matches. This method quickly becomes a solution to most recurring health problems. If there is a perfect match, and the ailment belongs to the category of most recurring health problems, prescriptions are ordered electronically so all the patient has to do is pick the medication up from the pharmacy.

This system fails if a match is not found or if it produces an extensive list. In such cases, the MRM system recommends a consultation with their doctor who then conducts an online consultation from the comfort of their home or office. The physician then recommends additional tests and/or a physical exam if needed. Once the patient is diagnosed and treated, the MRM database is updated to help future patients with similar symptoms. Over time, the size of the MRM database continues to grow and become much more sophisticated.

How does this MRM diagnosis affect the current cost of healthcare? Let me count the ways! One great benefit to this evolutionary adaptive healthcare system is the world becomes the target market. Anyone in the world could sign into this very affordable online healthcare system and be diagnosed. As no skilled labor force is physically involved here, the cost will be very affordable, keeping the quality and efficiency of diagnosis on par with the current market. Diagnosing most routine healthcare problems this way not only substantially reduces healthcare costs but increases the revenue considerably.

Patients in some developed areas of the world will not need to key in their medical history into the MRM, as most of their medical information is already be available online. However, patients from underdeveloped regions of the world may have to send their entire medical history at least once before diagnosis for a good match. Once sent, this information is stored online and updated when the patients use online diagnosis. All diagnoses and treatments go into an MRM database making the MRM more versatile and highly cost effective.

What we are trying to achieve is a practical application of the principle of automation. This is a systematic storage of health information and subsequent mapping for diagnosis. The MRM software performs routine jobs efficiently without a break and is easy to access from all over the world.

GLOBAL IMPACT OF MRM ON THE COST OF HEALTHCARE

The benefits of MRM diagnosis are many. You have heard of getting a second opinion – how about getting a third, fourth, or fifth. In this case, for a nominal fee set by physicians and hospitals, the patient can obtain another objective, qualified diagnosis. This online diagnosis potentially caters to a population of several billion. The substantial revenue earned via an MRM system helps bring down the cost and increases the quality of healthcare. The other great benefit of an MRM diagnosis is that once established it initiates mass-production of diagnostic tools.

The "MRM station" is another futuristic concept that renders services to collect blood and urine samples and/or scan specific parts of the body for analysis. The MRM system then receives the data from these stations. The MRM stations might initially host basic machines. Later on, as the system spreads around the world, it adds more sophisticated diagnostics as they became economically viable.

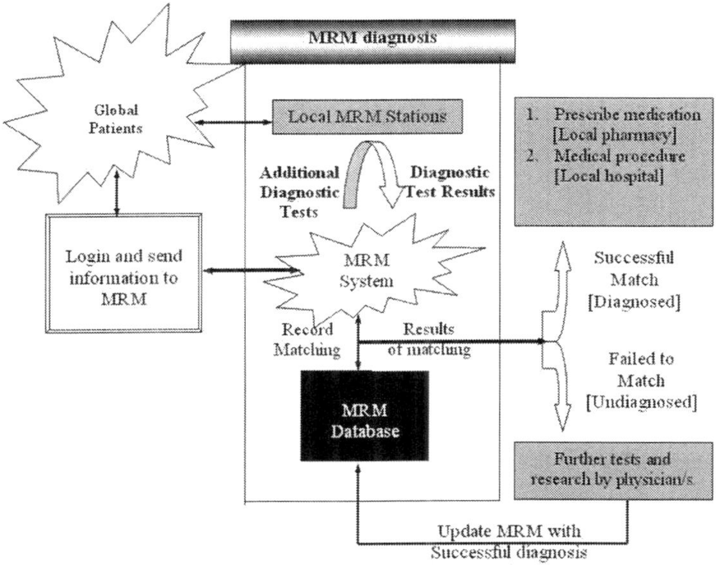

Fig 11: MRM Diagnosis

Establishing online diagnosis in the market creates demand for **MRM** stations around the world. This also creates demand for a multitude of businesses to produce the diagnostic tools.

Globalizing these products makes them more affordable to many entrepreneurs looking to open new MRM stations. The reduction in cost further increases the size of the market, as more people are able to afford it. This initiates the "positive feedback loop" of globalization in the healthcare industry. Even the pharmaceutical companies can sell more medicine, which helps them earn more revenue and invest more in further research. This will trigger a mega pharmaceutical industry. As the world's standard of living increases, more money will flow into the healthcare industry and create solutions where there were once only problems.

This new online system helps healthcare industry in the United States by reducing the number of annual doctor visits, eliminating the wait for a doctor's appointment, getting a diagnosis in a matter of minutes without leaving home, and substantially lowering healthcare costs. The implications for elderly patients, comprising a significant population in many countries, are obvious. Moreover, patients can get several opinions at the same time.

Hospitals and doctors benefit from the MRM diagnostic system by earning more money without spending any time with patients. In addition, unclogging this evolutionary bottleneck frees doctors to concentrate on critical patients that need personal care.

In many cities, the scarcity of doctors forces patients to wait months for an appointment. With this system in place, patients benefit because they get immediate diagnosis and doctors benefit because they are not spending as much time on routine colds or cuts and scrapes.

SETTING UP MRM SYSTEM

An MRM diagnosis matches the patient's symptoms and diagnostic test results with previously diagnosed cases. From a physician's perspective, setting up an MRM diagnosis is not an easy task. Physicians will have to input the patient's medical records and successful diagnoses to build an "MRM Database" used for easy mapping.

Today, in many developed countries, healthcare systems extensively use Information Technology and most of the medical records are being converted to electronic formats. In that sense, the MRM is already taking shape. As this grows bigger in size, MRM diagnoses become much more practical.

The larger the volume of medical records, the better the chances of hitting the right scenario. If a patient goes online with certain symptoms, the chances of matching their symptoms with an existing case are very high using a database containing a billion or more records. On the other hand, if the case is unique, a match may not be possible as there may not be any such cases documented. The online diagnosis system will reject such unique cases and doctors will have to manually diagnose and treat the disease. Once diagnosed the MRM updates and becomes much more useful for such unique cases.

Since certain diseases are specific to particular parts of the world, patients will benefit by the MRM correctly identifying such cases, matched with the right demographic area.

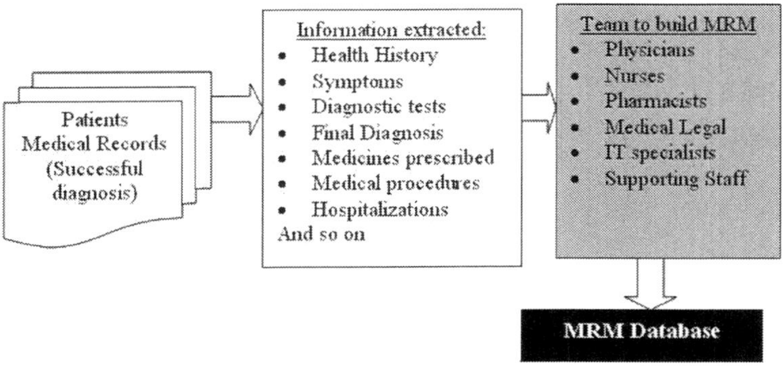

Fig 12: MRM Building Team

CONTINUOUS UPDATE OF MRM

A successful online diagnosis depends on the amount of records and on the latest information contained in the MRM databases. To assure this, MRM managers will continuously update their databases and increase its sophistication. MRM frees doctors from routine work and gives them an opportunity to research and diagnose diseases across the world, updating the MRM databases.

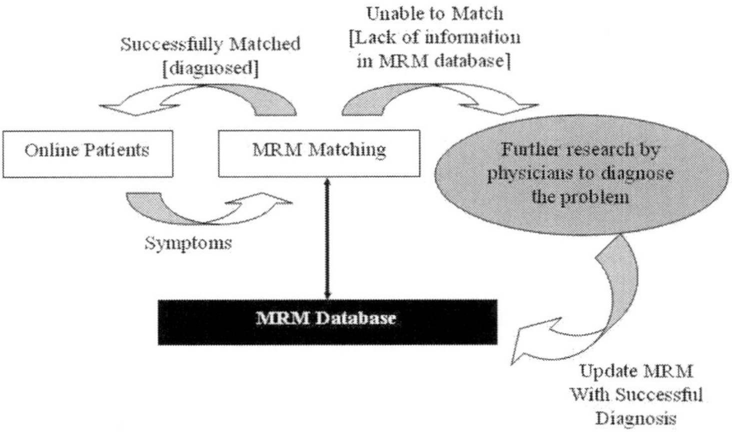

Fig 13: Continuous Update of MRM

Obviously, large hospitals and physicians' groups will have their MRM databases accessed the most heavily. As they grow, the databases will give more accurate results. However, smaller hospitals and medical groups will compete by offering other useful features like personal review of cases, one-on-one online discussions, and so on.

As time goes by, consolidation of these individual MRM databases will happen that will enable large and small hospitals groups to share revenue generated by the access.

IMPACT OF MRM ON PRIVATE AND GOVERNMENT CONTROLLED HEALTHCARE

In countries where private insurance companies manage healthcare, MRM technology will become inevitable to reduce costs. It is not a question of whether (or if) such technologies could arrive, but a question of when it will happen. Just like any other industry, when the cost becomes too unbearable, automation finds its own alternative ways. Private insurance companies will embrace this strategy much more easily than the government controlled healthcare systems, as the decisions are made by the company CEOs rather than a multitude of government regulatory layers.

In countries where the government manages healthcare, risky patients and expensive treatments overwhelm the system eventually, making online diagnosis the inevitable solution. Citizens will also embrace online healthcare and diagnosis because of its ease, no wait access, low cost and of course access to multiple opinions and instant access to ever changing healthcare technology.

'WEB MEDICINE' OF THE FUTURE

In underdeveloped regions of the world lacking good hospitals, using MRM diagnosis and MRM stations could eliminate the bottleneck caused by doctors' "physical presence" during diagnosis. We could make that information flow between doctor and patient for minimal cost.

As technology matures and the market improves, the MRM stations of the future will become more sophisticated and offer a variety of routine procedures and scans. Expensive procedures are greatly responsible for the high cost of today's healthcare so automating them using sophisticated machines will drastically reduce the cost. The huge revenue generated by the MRM system will fund research that further improves the technology going forward.

In the future, doctors' visits will be rare and hospital visits reserved for emergencies and other advanced medical complications. Machines will handle all routine procedures the world over.

The MRM concept is just the beginning of a long evolutionary chain leading to technologically advanced healthcare, leaving the Current Age far behind. Over time, as technology becomes more sophisticated, tests like CAT scans and MRIs will be available to patients 24/7 at these cutting-edge MRM stations.

Very soon, many home health-monitoring devices that can collect patient data such as blood pressure, pulse reading, glucose reading, eye scan, and so on, will emerge onto the market. They will interact with the MRM systems for a faster flow of information and collect data from the comfort of the patient's home. While some technologies already exist in the market, the future devices will collect increasingly detailed information in less time.

Ideally, the production of home health-monitoring devices will become a thriving industry, opening up massive employment opportunities for skilled people, while at the same time moving us out of the Current Age and into our next evolutionary phase.

MRM diagnosis, MRM stations, and home health-monitoring devices will initiate a machine-managed healthcare, which will take our health standard to an even higher level by replacing most human interaction with patient-machine interaction – the birth of web medicine. While it may seem like science fiction now, the introduction of machines in healthcare is inevitable as we continue to lower costs and improve the effectiveness of the healthcare system.

The automation of the healthcare industry affects the flow of medical information. Hospitals around the world will have instant access to every new breakthrough, diagnosis, and treatment because healthcare will exist on a connected global network. The machines will instantly assimilate new information, as it is available, keeping the network automatically updated. If a new epidemic hits a region of the world, its symptoms and needed treatment become instantly available to the global healthcare system, so the whole world benefits from this instant flow of information. As MRM keeps track of the health of the individuals, it is possible to track the spread of the epidemic in real time.

If all the money now spent on routine checkups and meaningless paper work goes into intellectual research, we will quickly attain a higher health standard in a short period. This concept is at the heart of what holds us back in the Current Age. Letting machines take over more and more of our routine jobs frees us to stop working so hard and start working smarter – the only move assured to take us into that safer future.

MRM AND MEDICAL STUDENTS

MRM will also help medical students to figure out what diagnosis an experienced physician would have suggested for particular patient. Even for experienced physicians, this will give them more confidence in whatever diagnosis and treatment they are suggesting. They can quickly scan thru all similar cases and find out how they were diagnosed and treated in different hospitals around the world.

IMPACT OF MRM ON MALPRACTICE INSURANCE

Medical malpractice insurance is in place to maintain high-quality healthcare. Doctors and hospitals pay huge premiums to cover any human error that results in a wrong diagnosis or treatment regimen that may eventually have severe, damaging, or even fatal results. This cost trickles down to the patients, resulting in higher healthcare costs for all involved.

A good medical diagnosis depends on precise lab tests. While more lab tests lead to higher healthcare costs, fewer lab tests can lead to the wrong diagnosis, resulting in exorbitant legal costs and malpractice claims. Either way, patients are the ones penalized. An MRM system is a simple solution to this problem, as under this model, frequent tests will not add to the healthcare costs, as the diagnostic machines are mass-produced and are very affordable. As a result, more tests and better diagnoses eventually reduce the cost of malpractice insurance.

JUNK FOOD TO HEALTHY FOOD

Whether we eat in a restaurant or buy food in a supermarket, to the majority of the population, cost is one of the driving factors when deciding what to buy, when, where, and even how often. Since it is often more expensive to eat in a sit-down restaurant – particularly for a family of four, for instance – junk food and generally unhealthy choices often win over healthy food based on cost. Junk food quite is also often tastier than its healthier counterpart, and there is no incentive to choose a healthier food alternative.

For example, a bag of chips costs a dollar or less, while the same size fresh salad costs two to three times that amount. This bottom-heavy analysis of healthy food versus junk food has literally changed the food habits of an entire generation of Americans, resulting in obesity, diabetes, and other long-term health issues at very young ages.

It is also not always possible to keep track of the calories or the kind of food we eat. Often, it is hard to figure out how many calories are in each menu item. The effects of over-eating are slow to manifest themselves, and many only notice a health condition like obesity or diabetes or heart disease after several years – or even decades. When these people visit doctors and receive treatment in a hospital, the cost of healthcare goes up.

It all comes down to money. Insurance companies will save a fortune if people are healthy. "Real-time health monitoring" can easily find solutions to these types of medical issues. With automation in health monitoring, we will soon wear monitoring devices to test our blood and monitor our food intake. Affordable, simple, and practical devices like blood sugar monitors, for example, allow people to get immediate feedback on their blood chemistry.

Insurance companies could give discounts for people who wear these machines and prove they are eating healthy. Like motorists attending defensive driving classes, or a teenager maintaining a GPA of 4.0 to obtain discounts on auto insurance, anyone not wearing this device will pay more for insurance. With this system, we would find a huge demand for these machines and companies competing to produce state of the art products to help people monitor their blood chemistry with as much less discomfort as possible. The current non-prick devices will soon get more sophisticated for regular usage.

AUTOMATION IN RESTAURANTS

Many restaurants are already listing nutritional information on their menu. In the future this becomes a necessity so people can choose the right food and right quantity to suit their health.

Even the monitoring devices themselves will soon evolve to track this information and advise you on the menu selection. Instead of a restaurant menu, you will watch the screen of your monitoring device, which already has the restaurant menu and makes several recommendations to suit your daily intake. Picking from this recommended list, your food intake will match your daily needs and the monitor that samples your blood, will reflect this information, which will be sent to your health insurance company in real time.

With this system, restaurants will be extra cautious in what they serve their customers, with emphasis on food items on their menu that are easily picked up by the monitoring devices. Soon, it will not be our palate that controls what we eat, but insurance companies in an attempt to keep us healthy. Prevention rather than cure will be their business focus.

This system will not only be a great service to the general public, but will also help by boosting the evolutionary pace with healthy and long-living individuals who have literally evolved from the "Junk Food Era" to the "Healthy Food Era."

CHAPTER 11

EVOLUTIONARY SOLUTION TO THE ECONOMIC RECESSION

THE "THREE DEVILS" OF ECONOMIC RECESSION

The stock bubble, housing bubble, and energy bubble are the three undesirable forces responsible for any economic recession. Even though each one of these events is capable of causing serious economic damage, when they hit us at the same time, the effects are felt worldwide. This is exactly what happened during the 2008 recession. When the housing market collapsed in 2006, risky credit began to hurt the stock market, which stumbled in 2008. Oil prices were then at their peak, as the economy was booming. This energy-inflicted inflation began to hurt the real economy even more, causing the inevitable recession. This is what I refer as the "Meeting of the Three Devils."

THE HOUSING BUBBLE:

In the graph below, we see prices have steadily risen during 2006 that resulted in a market crash. This housing bubble affected the entire world during 2006.

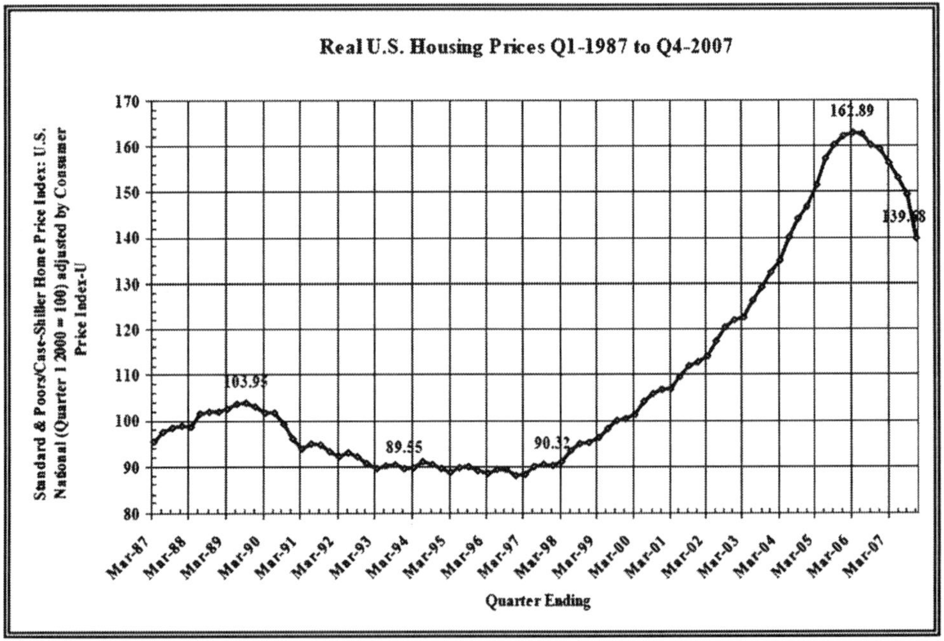

Fig 14: Real U.S. Housing Prices Q1-1987 to Q4-2007

Source: The U.S. Housing Bubble and the Global Financial Crisis: Housing and Housing-Related Finance. -By Ranking Republican Member Jim Saxton (R-NJ) - Joint Economic Committee - United States Congress May 2008

With the real estate market becoming global, people are not limited to their own country for investments. It is very common to see people residing in one country while buying property in other countries for investment purposes. Real estate entrepreneurs have invested in multiple countries. In a global perspective, we see a common trend in the real estate market in most developed countries, where a rise or decline in price affects investors in several countries at the same time. Whether these price adjustments cause a market crash will depend on the number of people affected and their capability to survive the fall. The more their survival capabilities are the less impact the crash will have on the economy. However, if it affects the standard of living for a significant number of people, then it becomes a real market crash.

If we can find out why there was a sharp rise in price, we can create a solution for such market crashes in the future. In upcoming chapters, we look at the real estate market from the evolutionary perspective to find real world solution.

THE STOCK MARKET BUBBLE

The graph below shows the performance of the major global stock indexes from 2000 to 2009.

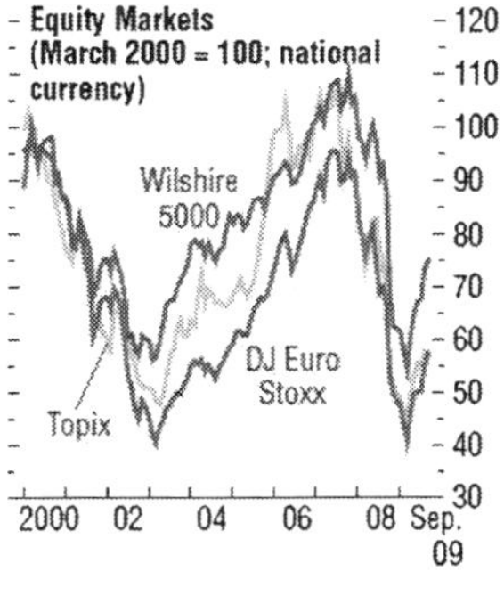

Fig 15 Major Stock Indexes from 2000-2009

Source: IMF - International Monetary Fund - World Economic Outlook-Sustaining the Recovery October 2009 (Chapter1 Global Prospects and Policies - P5, Figure 1.3. Developments in Mature Credit Markets)

Permission to publish: Ref#3716498 date: 12-15-10

THE ENERGY BUBBLE:

The graph below shows the energy prices at their peak before the recession began.

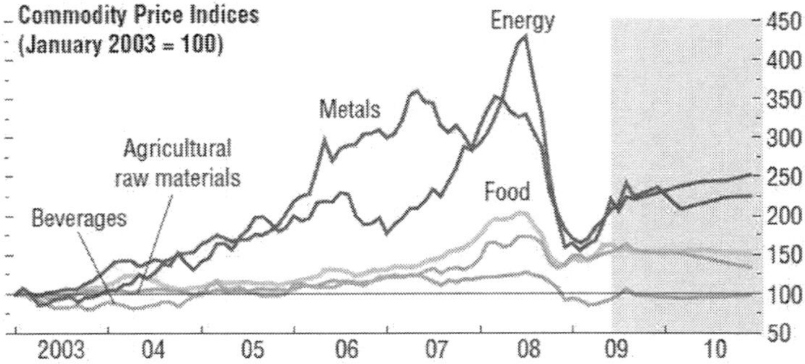

Fig 16 Energy and Commodity Prices 2003-2009

Source: IMF – International Monetary Fund – World Economic Outlook-Sustaining the Recovery October 2009- (Chapter1 Global Prospects and Policies – P50, Appendix 1.1,Figure 1.16)
Authors: Kevin Cheng, Nese Erbil, Thomas Helbling, Shaun Roache, and Marina Rousset.
Permission to publish: Ref#3716498 date: 12-15-10

Although many economists did spot these bubbles, they failed to understand their severity. These bubbles exist because of a lack of information flow in the system coupled with our inability to regulate the market. We may not be able to change human nature, but we can regulate our economy appropriately, not by imposing rules and regulations that can be broken, but via automation. In upcoming chapters, we look at each of these bubbles from the evolutionary perspective to find real world solution.

CHAPTER 12

EVOLUTIONARY SOLUTION TO THE ENERGY CRISIS

THE CRISIS

Among the three resources, **R**aw materials, **E**nergy, and **L**abor (**REL**), the most important resource for any industry to operate is "Energy." This is a major factor, which currently poses, and has been posing, a threat to our flourishing economy.

We begin by understanding this energy source from a macroscopic point of view. Solar energy comes to our planet in the form of sunlight. All plants on earth store this energy through photosynthesis. Herbivorous animals get this energy by eating plants. In turn, carnivorous animals eat animals for energy.

It would be accurate to say all living beings on earth derive energy either directly or indirectly from the sun.

When we move our finger, it is the solar energy actually moving it. Solar energy flows in all of us. Why then did our search for energy begin with digging for fossil fuel? Why did not we invest in this great source of energy? Did lobbyists mislead us?

The answer, of course, lies in our technological evolution itself. We can trace our current dependency on non-solar energy back to our very first engine that, as you will recall from history textbooks in grade school, was a steam-powered engine, not a solar-powered engine.

During that time, our knowledge of utilizing solar energy was primitive at best and nonexistent at worst. The world celebrated the invention of the first steam engine because it was the greatest evolutionary product of that time. We embraced the technology and our economy began building on this energy source almost immediately. Capitalizing on this technology, we were able to move many more goods quickly, evolving at a steady rate. Gradually, coal power became the backbone of our economy.

We ate solar food, but traveled on coal! Isn't it ironic?

Then came oil, a more sophisticated source for almost all of our energy needs. In spite of its sophistication, it has not totally replaced coal even today. Coal is so deeply rooted in our economy that to this day there are hundreds of active coalmines around the world.

Literally thousands of coal miners around the world are still working hard to mine the fabled "black gold." The energy generation from both coal and oil is very well established and both are quite vast sources. The sad part however is neither source support a sudden surge in energy demand.

The alternative sources of energy like solar, wind, hydro, geothermal, and tidal are quite recent and still in early development. These sources cannot compete with established sources like coal and oil, at their present stage of evolution. The technology behind them is not sophisticated enough for mass production, so they have remained alternatives and have not become primary sources.

Coal and oil, have ruled the world for a long time. We have dug, burrowed, and mined our planet to our heart's content. The impact is nothing short of catastrophic. It is not only global warming we are concerned about, but also the non-sustainable form of energy source on which our global economy depends.

The data below shows the dominance of fossil fuel over other sources in the world.

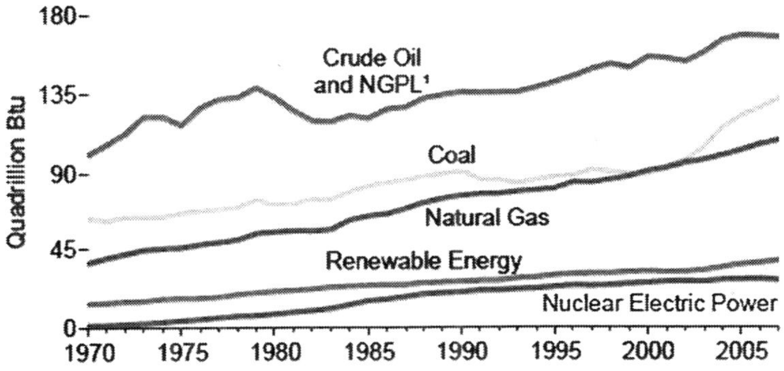

Fig 17: World Primary Energy Production by Source

Source: U.S. Energy Information Administration, Annual Energy Review 2009: Energy Perspectives: 1949-2009 Report No. DOE/EIA-0384(2009): Release Date: August 19, 2010.
Note: [1]Natural gas plant liquids

To find a solution to this energy crisis, let us use our evolutionary principles. The invention criterion for this industry is "production and supply of energy." Initially this industry started with very primitive thermal power plants using coal from small mines. Even the oilrigs that extracted oil were very small. As more industries emerged, the market size for energy increased. This market demand put a lot of pressure on the quantity of energy generated. The demand for more power gave rise to the evolution criterion **"throughput."**

To satisfy this criterion, the energy industry responded by building larger thermal power plants and more oil refineries. The shipping and transportation industry expanded as well to transport coal and oil. Each thermal power plant came with a huge investment in coalmines and each refinery needed multiple oilrigs. The profits were also equally high. Energy companies earned substantial revenue selling energy.

As the global economy expanded, demand for energy increased so much the energy industry was unable to meet the demand quickly enough. It takes years and decades to build thermal power plants and refineries. The sudden increase in demand and insufficient supply caused the cost to rise. Our immediate responsibility should be to address the evolution criterion **"throughput"** to meet this high demand.

The reason we are not able to move away from oil and coal dependency is we do not have adequate technology to use other sources of energy efficiently...yet. The technology behind non-conventional sources has grown very slowly with little appreciable progress.

The other factor that is of greatest concern is the participation of developing and underdeveloped countries in the global economy. These countries have begun to consume considerable energy, especially oil and coal. Should these countries develop slowly until we find a good energy source? Not unless we want to remain stagnant in this slow current global economy! Our planet needs more industries to evolve faster. We need more underdeveloped countries to develop to support the growing economy.

Let us use the principle of automation to ease the throughput bottleneck. We have two possible options: We can apply this principle to the existing source or we can start from scratch with a new source. If we apply the principle of automation to our existing coal mines, thermal power plants, oil rigs, and oil refineries, we can eliminate the human element and replace them with efficient machines and robots that will not only do a faster, more efficient job but could be replicated to build more power plants simultaneously. This will improve the supply and the cost will decrease substantially. However, sources (oil and coal) themselves are being depleted and causing ecological problems.

Back when we first struck oil, we knew oil would one day be depleted. Still we celebrated it and built mega industries around this non-sustainable source. Entrepreneurs may or may not take us on the right path; they are there to compete and succeed by supplying new products and services. It is the responsibility of governments to make the appropriate policies and guide economic growth in the right direction. This is where all governments around the world failed. The more prudent path is not only to switch to solar energy but to automate the process of building the solar power plant.

The sun has so much energy that merely capturing an infinitely small fraction of it will make us energy sufficient. Tapping into such a mega source is the wisest decision we could ever make.

INTRODUCING RAP (ROBOT-AIDED-PRODUCTION) METHODOLOGY

RAP is a process of adapting automation in every job in the entire production plant. It is a collection of a multitude of partial automations. Partial automation exists in our current industries and need not be invented from scratch. For example, in the beverage industry, bottling jobs are already automated; in the automobile industry, robots are already handling some precision assembly. RAP would greatly benefit from existing automation technologies, although it is not sufficient to build a completely automated RAP plant.

The usage of robots in industry will not happen unless the ROI (return on investment) is profitable. Robots are still very expensive and automation of production units requires both time and money. This is the reason many businesses, including energy producing companies, still use manual labor and struggle to increase their throughput. RAP would kick start the automation ahead of time to exploit the great benefits the machines have to offer.

One of the greatest benefits of RAP is its ability to replicate. This is exactly what we need in the energy industry today. We will be able to produce as much energy as needed and as quickly as possible by replication and not by building power plants from scratch. Several solar power plants have been built in the world from scratch, each one a massive project. Transferring these skills to other humans via training is quite a task.

The robots, however, will keep all the programmed skills and take the stress, anxiety, and human error out of training and teaching workers to do the repeatable skills a robot could do both precisely and continuously.

Now let us see how we can use this RAP concept to the solar power plant industry, one we will heavily rely on in the Age of Automation. If we apply RAP to individual processes, like manufacturing solar cells, assembling solar panels, the transportation of these panels to a power plant site, and finally to the assembly of a solar power plant on site, then we will end up with a fully automated "Power Plant building industry," which can sustain itself and could be replicated when needed. "Solar Power Plants" will now become the end product of this massive RAP industry. In essence, automation transforms mega projects into products of RAP industries that can be mass-produced.

These robots, once programmed to do specific tasks, will keep doing them tirelessly until the power plant assembly was complete. Initially, of course, the cost will be very high, as highly skilled labor to plan, build, and program these robots is needed. We might even need substantial energy from fossil fuels to build such a plant. After the completion of the first plant, however, the entire army of robots will build another solar power plant, an exact replica of the first, in another designated location, by themselves.

There will be no further need to start the process from scratch or enlist human talent to design or redesign new blueprints or drawings. In fact, no skill transfer will be needed, period. All the information fed into these robots during the first power plant would be reused in the second plant, except perhaps for some new information about the topography of the second site.

Robots will even get their energy from the first solar power plant and will become self-reliant once it is operational. After completion of the second power plant and after making sure the automated process is working without much intervention from humans, we could **replicate** the entire army of robots to build several power plants in parallel.

Imagine an army of robots producing solar power plants one after another without much human physical involvement. Imagine an industry that could produce such an army of robots continuously. Within a short time, we would end up with thousands of power plants all over the world, all built and managed by robots.

Although this process is fully automated, these RAP industries need enormous skilled human labor to monitor the robots and to redesign or reprogram them for better efficiency. These robots go through continuous improvement as humans make them better day after day. This is how the industry will technologically evolve into the future.

The ultimate benefit of RAP is its quick replication capability to produce power upon demand, eliminating the"**throughput"** bottleneck.

The diagram below shows production of RAP machines and their evolution.

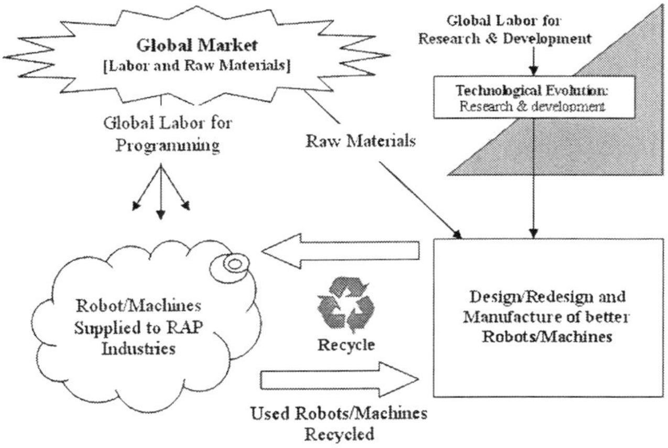

Fig 18: Producing RAP machines

The diagram below shows usage of RAP in solar power plants

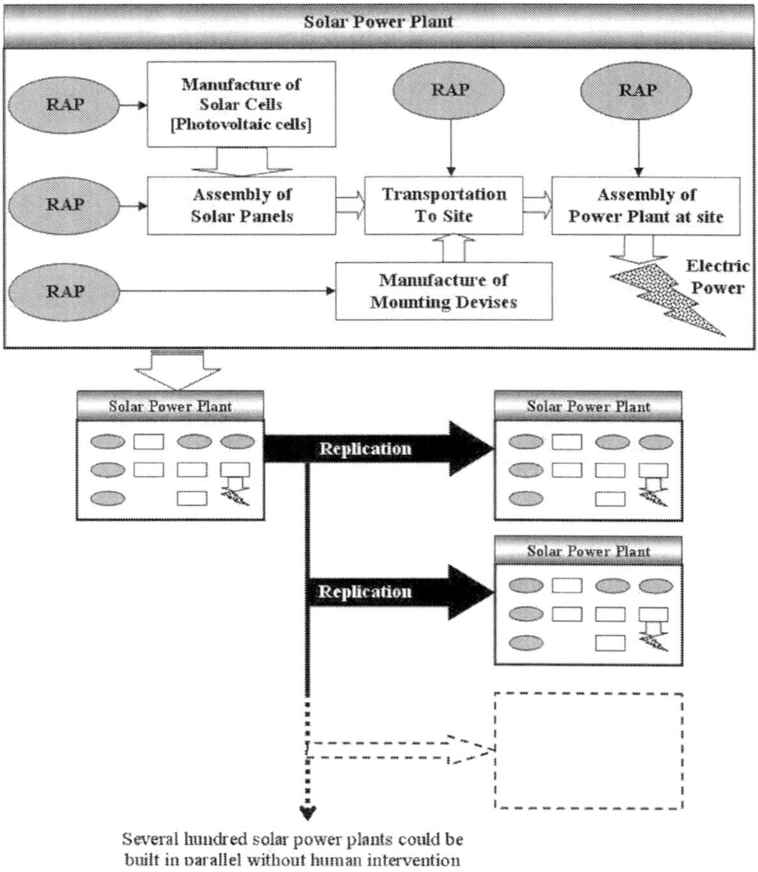

Fig 19: Using RAP in Solar Power Plant

What will be the cost of electricity produced by this industry? It will be the cheapest possible; the cheapest, in fact, we have ever paid for such a plentiful and reliable energy supply. As technology behind solar cells becomes even more sophisticated, solar energy will become the most affordable on the planet, taking the global economy to new heights.

By the time we reach the end of the Age of Automation, energy will literally be free. Like ants building ant-nests or bees building honeycombs without any human effort, RAP plants grow in number without any human intervention. This is level-1 automation. In level 2 and 3, they will begin to advance themselves as discussed under the principle of automation.

Once the robot-manufacturing industry establishes itself, robots will be very affordable and other businesses will naturally start adapting RAP methodology. The biggest impact of this will be on raw materials. Since mining companies use manual labor and expensive energy, the raw materials are very expensive. With cheap energy, the raw materials will become very affordable. When the miners adapt the RAP method, the raw materials will become even more affordable. Wood, steel, aluminum, plastic, and a host of other materials will become very low cost, making our end products inexpensive. This accelerates the "positive feedback loop" of globalization discussed earlier. The living standard of people proportionately rises moving us towards the Age of Automation much faster.

Compare the RAP approach to the manual approach currently employed. Expensive human labor is involved in producing solar cells, assembly into solar panels, and designing and building solar power plants. This labor-intensive process not only makes the production slow and inefficient, but extremely expensive. The same methodology is used in other energy producing industries too. The thermal plants, oilrigs and refineries are heavily dependent on skilled manual labor.

Moreover, after completion of a power plant, the industry starts over again from scratch to build another. Transfer of knowledge is inefficient, too, especially when an employee quits or retires.

RAP, on the other hand, will be the fastest way to produce not just energy, but any product in the world. To survive global disasters, we need to move at a good pace with our technological evolution. If the private companies shy away from this task for financial reasons, the governments must act and take the full initiative of adapting the RAP concept in the energy sector.

As RAP involves time-consuming research work, a start has to be made now. This is also a great opportunity to create jobs and establish a new industry sector.

CHAPTER 13

EVOLUTIONARY SOLUTION TO THE STOCK MARKET CRISIS

WHY STOCK BUBBLES HURT US

A stock introduced into the market for ten dollars may soon trade at a hundred dollars or more simply because people think the company is a success and a moneymaker. The fictitious value of the stock could be sky high, even though there is little or no substantial change in the companies to which these stocks belong. The industries are still the same, but their stock values have gone up just because people compete to buy them. This deviation of the price of stock from the real price causes what is known in financial circles as "bubbles." These unreal prices would be just waiting for a chance to bite the stockholders. Any stock market growth, which is beyond the rate at which the real economy is growing, gives rise to bubbles. The more the prices of such investments deviate from reality, the bigger the bubble. If more people are involved in such investments, thicker will be the bubble, which means, if the bubble bursts, more people are affected—both the size and the thickness of the bubble matters.

This chapter focuses more on understanding the evolutionary nature of stock trading rather than the technicalities of the stock trading.

Now, let's look at stock trading from an evolutionary angle. People invest in stocks for only one reason, to grow their investment along with the real economic growth. However, bubbles form invariably as these stock prices do not really reflect the true value of the company to which those stocks belong.

When the investors realize the actual value of the stock has gone much beyond the real price, the bubble bursts. There is panic selling of stocks and the stock market plummets. In many stock market crashes, the indexes have dropped more than 30 percent in one day. Remember, there is little or no substantial change in the companies to which these stocks belong.

Those who sell their stocks quickly make profit; others lose by responding too slowly, if at all. As the stock market crash is always sudden, only a few will be able to sell their stocks in time. During a stock market crash, most people lose and only a few people get rich. What really happens during a crash is a simple transfer of money from losers to gainers.

In the United States, there have been several stock market crashes; some of the notable ones were in 1929, 1987, 2000, and 2008.

Even though there are considerable price fluctuations and market crashes, the overall value of stocks keep increasing over time

The following graph shows the growth of Dow Jones (DJI) since 1900s.

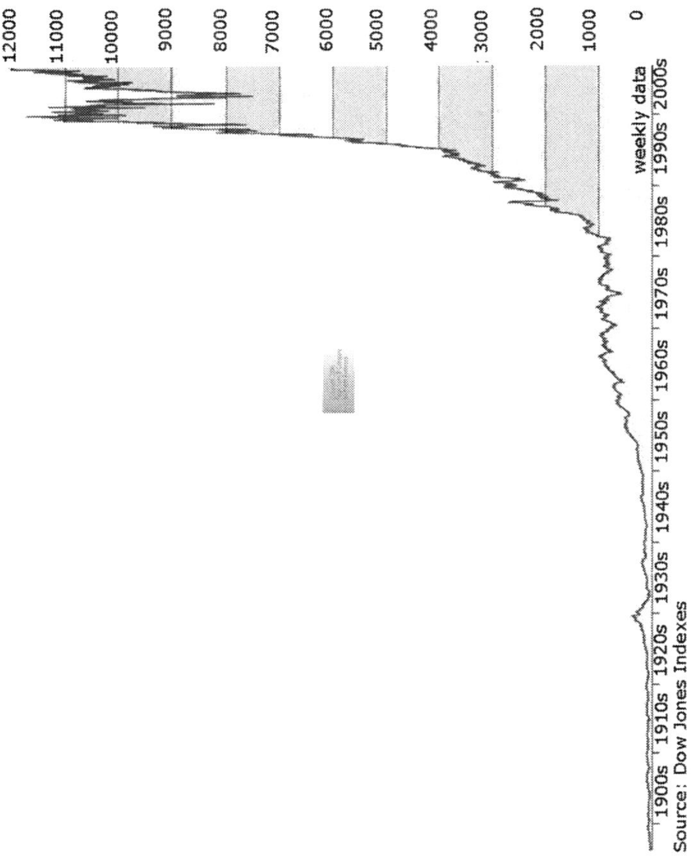

Fig 20: Stock Market Growth of Dow Jones (DJI) from 1900s to 2000s Source: Dow Jones and Company, Inc. Reprints License Number: 2565420008472

If in spite of bubbles and crashes, the stock market continues to grow, why should we be concerned about these crashes?

From an evolutionary perspective, what we should be concerned with are not the crashes themselves, but their effect on the investors, potentially decreasing their standard of living and the eventual affect on the industries. Every time the stock market dips, while some people make money, many lose money. We are concerned about people who lost their money. They are the ones who will affect the economy negatively. Those who made the profit will not affect the economy positively enough to offset these negative effects. Looking from an evolutionary angle, we should focus on the change in living standard of a vast section of the population when the stock market plummets.

Let us look at the relation between the economy and our standard of living to understand the effect of stock market crash even better. It is very interesting to see how the entire economy is dependent on how we spend. Our standard of living is so important for the economy, that if our spending habit is affected, it in turn affects a whole network of industries. The following data from the United States Bureau of Labor Statistics shows how much we have been spending all these years.

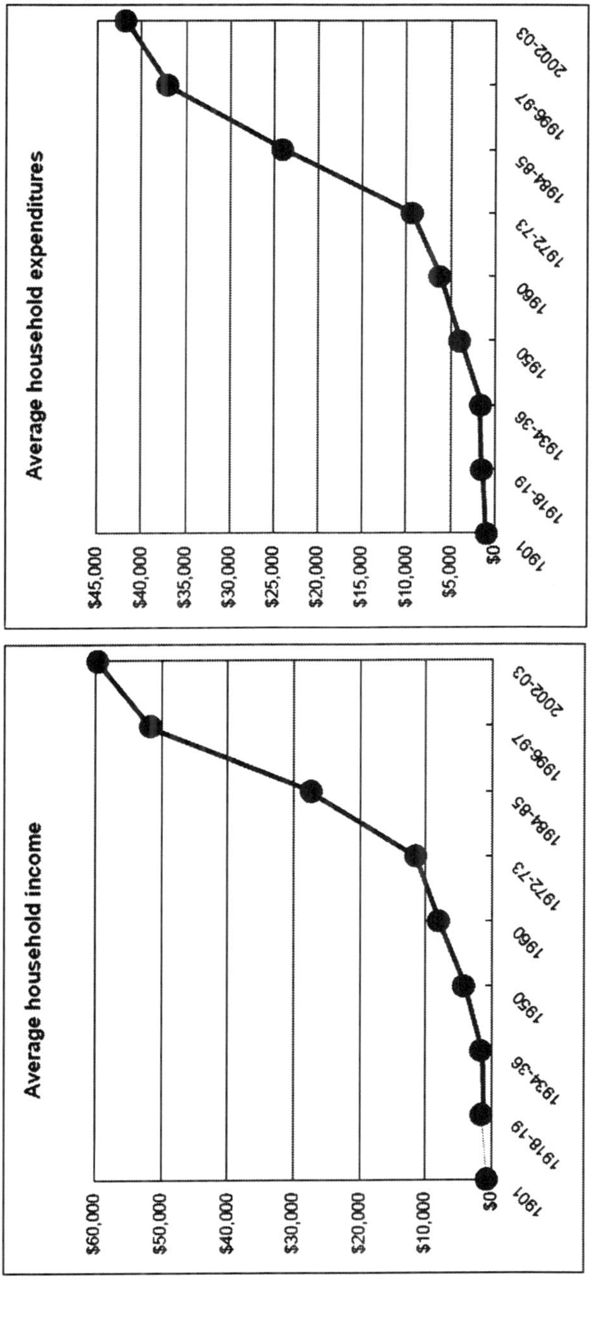

Fig 21: Economic and demographic indicators, U.S. 2002-03

Source: U.S. Bureau of Labor Statistics, Consumer Expenditure Survey, and U.S. Census Bureau, Statistical Abstract of the United State – 100 Years of U.S. Consumer Spending

From the above graphs, we can see for the past one hundred years, both our income and spending has gradually increased. Industries have grown proportionate to this spending habit. Any small change in our lifestyle could potentially bankrupt many industries. For example, if we slow down vacationing, it would seriously affect the travel industry and smaller businesses might even collapse. For instance, an average American family spends about $1,000 during the summer holiday season each year – for a working population of 150 million, this equates to $150 billion. If they spend one dollar less, it will be $150 million less for the economy. Such is the dependency of the economy on our spending habits.

The fact is, if people's spending habits do not change during a stock market crash, the economy will not go into recession. From an evolutionary angle, every one of us plays a very significant role in the economy. Wherever we invest, we have to make sure there is enough savings buffer so our standard of living will not drastically change when the economy plummets.

Though it is easy to say, it is not easy to put this into practice. Many people take risks and invest heavily in the stock market with little or no savings at all. Many people think it is their own money and they can do whatever they want with it. They do not realize they are one among the other 150 million pillars that holds the economy in place. When the stock market crashes, risky investors may bring the real economy into recession.

To find a solution to this perpetual problem, we need to understand the evolutionary nature of our stock market.

EVOLUTION OF STOCK EXCHANGES

If we look at the stock exchanges from an evolutionary angle, they have followed all three criteria of the principle of desire: Invention/ Evolution (I/E), Quality, and Cost.

In the past, trades were done manually and trading volume was very low. As the demand for stocks increased, "availability" of tradable stocks became the evolution criteria. This "availability" has been and will be the driving force for future evolution of stock exchanges. To satisfy this evolution criterion, the number of exchanges has increased. Many existing exchanges have also expanded and added other trading products, including various derivatives.

To satisfy the "quality" criteria, the exchanges have made many rules and regulations to prohibit illegal trades committed knowingly or unknowingly. In the United States, after the 1929 crash the Government intervened and established the Securities Exchange Commission (SEC) to maintain the quality of trade. Most stock exchanges have regulatory departments of their own to track down trade violations. In addition, these stock exchanges have competed with each other thereby bringing down trading costs and further boosting the trading volume.

After the advent of computers, the exchanges took advantage of the electronic media to satisfy "availability" criteria to a greater extent. The exchanges were able to trade more stocks using Information Technology. Upon the advent of the Internet, exchanges became global trading centers (principle of globalization) and stocks of every industry across the world became available online. This globalization has resulted in huge trading volumes.

Soon "speed" became the evolution criteria. People wanted to trade stocks as quickly as they can. This made manual trading less and less effective.

Eventually, the exchanges became automated (principle of automation) so people can automate their trade online and trade any time of the day or night. Today, software of the stock exchanges matches most trades, and many times, there is no human involved.

Both globalization and automation have helped each other to evolve this stock trading industry into a mega industry as it stands today. If you look at stock exchanges as a service, they have followed all the evolutionary principles and could be considered highly evolved systems in a service industry.

Further, the evolution criterion "speed" has given rise to "high-speed trading," where millions of stocks are traded at fractions of a second. This high speed trading can identify both upward movement and downward movement of stocks every microsecond. This high speed trading is geared towards finding that ideal price of stock. This will be the path of all stock markets in the future, to find that most accurate price of stocks.

Let us discuss further how this high speed trading could evolve into the future satisfying our desire for continuous economic growth without any bubbles.

UNDERSTANDING THE STOCK BUBBLE

Primarily, investors invest in stocks that are making money. Now the question is how do they identify which stocks are making or will make money? We are all very familiar with stock price fluctuations. Stock prices fluctuate with the global markets. Global markets, on the other hand, fluctuate with the consumer behavior. For instance, if more people are buying houses, real estate values go up and the related company stocks go up. If there is more demand for oil, energy prices go up and Oil Company's stock goes up. The consumer behavior decides the price of the stocks. As stock prices normally point in the direction of consumer behavior, keeping an eye on global markets is as good as keeping an eye on the stock market.

Many times political news also affects the stock prices. This is when stock prices fail to reflect the global markets. Although information on consumer behavior that we discussed above is being used by the stock market, the flow of information not fast enough. Because of the lack of speed of availability of real-time information on consumer behavior, the stock market is becoming sensitive to all types of global information.

Traders are using stock trading as a means to find the best stock price. No one knows tomorrow's value of a stock until it is traded. Once traders depend on the trading itself as the mechanism to find the best stock price, the stock bubbles become inevitable.

What we need now to estimate the latest stock price is sophisticated Information Technology that can automate the process of collection of global financial information. When our Information Technology begins to supply the latest (real time) global financial data at high speed it will become a reliable source, on which the stock markets can depend.

CONSOLIDATED DATABASES:

As of today, every bank has its own database and has the ability to track its customer's financial activities. However, they lack a consolidated database that gives a feel of the global economy.

What is needed is a consolidation of these individual databases into one large national and eventually a global financial database (a futuristic concept), and sophisticated software that can track the financial transactions of every person and every industry in the nation and eventually in the world. Though this is a far-fetched idea, the future of stock trading has all the reason to go in this evolutionary path.

Here is how the Information Technology of the future will help us to ease the formation of stock bubbles. Highly sophisticated algorithms (or ALGO for short) will determine the stock price every nanosecond by sensing the latest and the greatest information about industries from global financial databases. They will use real time information and not days-old or months-old information. For instance, the moment we swipe our cards in a shopping mall, the ALGO will instantly capture the information of the transaction. If a company ships out a product, the ALGO will get the information. If a company pays its employees, the ALGO will get that information instantly. By continuously sniffing the market, ALGO will know every company's sales, market size, pending orders, expenses, and investments. Every transaction will be tracked globally and the ALGO will calculate the present worth of the company to the last penny every nanosecond and determine the very accurate stock price based on a universal algorithm. The details of this algorithm are out of scope of this book. However, this discussion is enough to visualize the evolutionary path of the stock market.

Once an accurate value of stock is determined, the bubbles become highly visible. As of today there are many indicators in the market, which approximately identifies the value of stocks. In the future, the same indicators will evolve further showing the stock prices with much more accuracy. Because of the absence of global consolidated database and lack of sophisticated software that can collect global data at high speeds, the stock market is currently depending on the trading mechanism to identify the value of stocks. In the process, it many times deviates too much from real economic growth, forming bubbles.

Bubbles will begin to dampen as and when our Information Technology gets more sophisticated. I believe this discussion will help us to visualize the evolutionary nature of the stock market, which is highly dependent on how fast our Information Technology flourishes.

The following diagram shows a typical consolidated database.

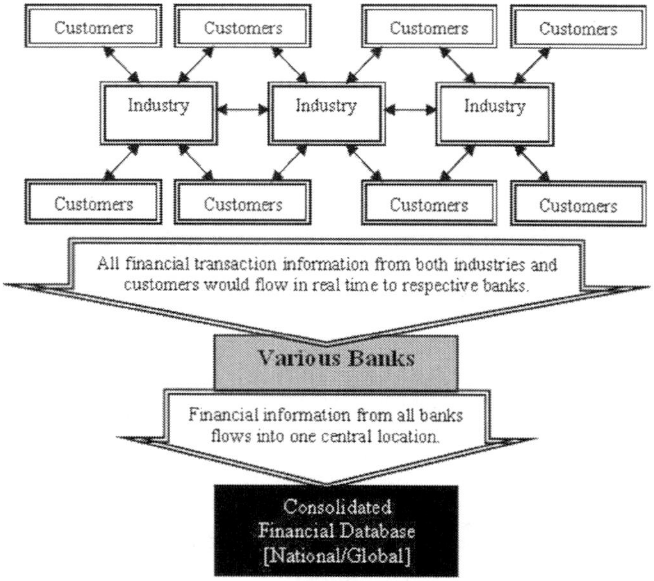

Fig 22: Building Consolidated Database

The diagram below shows how the consolidated database could be used to reduce bubbles in stock markets.

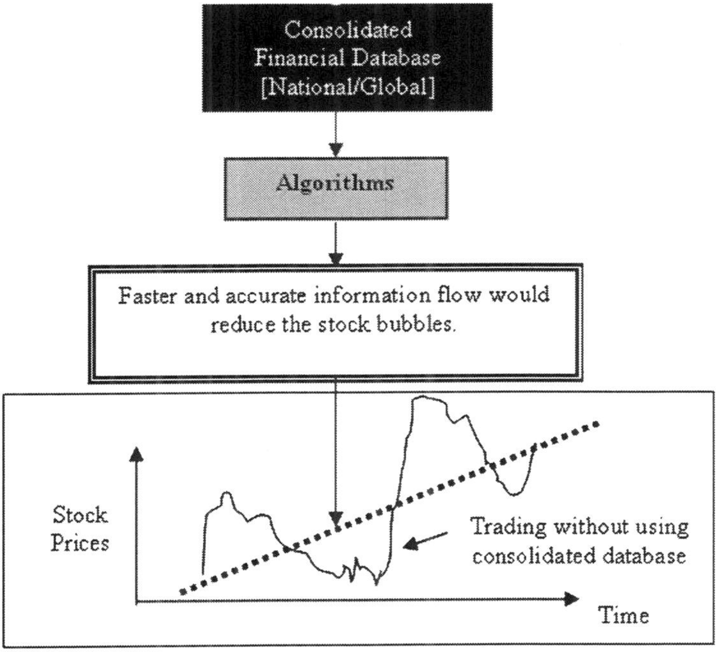

Fig 23: Using Consolidated Database to Reduce Stock Bubble

As we approach the Age of Automation, all financial transactions will become electronic, e-currency will become the currency of convenience, and hard currency will slowly fade away. No one can cash out their money and keep it under his/her pillow – a nasty habit in many countries, slowing the economy! When the world realizes hard currency only promotes illegal financial activities and is truly not needed for regular transactions, the printing of hard currency will stop. Those days are not far away; as our technology advances, they will take shape.

Elimination of hard currency helps the formation of consolidated databases quickly. Electronic devices will have evolved to meet the need for electronic transactions. We will use either our cell phone or some other electronic device to exchange money.

Creation of consolidated database will not dampen the high speed trading. In fact, high speed trading will continue to gain speed. However, trading will be much more focused on the economic growth rather than unrelated political or other information, in the sense that bubbles are almost non-existent. This will also put lot of pressure on companies to perform well to stay competitive.

Further into the future, to satisfy this human desire for high speed trading, trades will not happen in seconds but will happen at lightning speed. When our home computers and networks become fast, high speed trading will be the norm. By then we will have sophisticated software that can manage our investments. With bubble free economy, we can all focus on our jobs and careers, rather than stock trading to make quick money creating bubbles.

As bubbles fade out, every one of us will invest in stocks to grow our investment. Information technology will continue to grow capturing the financial data at high speed and stock market will eventually become a safe, reliable investment platform, which I would like to call as "stock cloud," which contains all stocks in the world. Every penny earned in the world will always be in the cloud. This will mean all our money is always invested in the economy and grows with the economy with no bubble formation. Stock and the currency will become the two faces of the global economy.

High speed trading that is happening today is a step toward the formation of such a mega financial system.

How quickly we reach that stage depends on how quickly our currency become electronic and global databases are created, which in turn is dependent on the pace of globalization. As globalization creates more economic activity, it will invariably put pressure on these two aspects. High economic pace creates demand for the electronic currency. This e-currency makes it easy for global databases to take shape.

Pace of globalization is paramount to reach the advanced world. As we contemplate more, we will find that "pace of globalization" is the most important solution to most problems of the current world.

CHAPTER 14

EVOLUTIONARY SOLUTION TO THE REAL ESTATE CRISIS

UNDERSTANDING THE HOUSING BUBBLE

Homes, although built primarily to live in, have become investment properties as well. Many people bought homes with the idea of making money while living in it. It is a dream not just to own a home but also to grow that investment. As prices rose, many homeowners became serious investors and started buying second and third homes as investments. There is nothing wrong with such investments as long as folks can afford them. However, this caused more demand in the housing market and prices started climbing because of a fictional perception these homes were actually worth the inflated amount.

Here again **easy credit** or bad loans play their gruesome role. The value of United States sub-prime mortgages was estimated at $1.3 trillion as of March 2007.

In a booming market, even if the homeowner is unable to pay, the home value will have appreciated and the banks will recoup their money by selling those homes in the event borrowers default on the loan. In a seller's market, even if the homeowners are a credit risk, the houses themselves are not. This is one of the reasons for promoting easy credit.

Below is a graph showing the United States home price variations from 1988-2008.

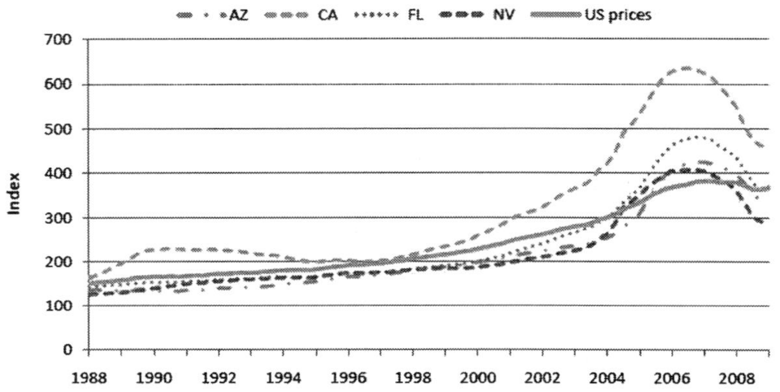

Fig 24: House Price Appreciation by Selected States

Source: Federal Housing Finance Agency: January 1980-100

This speculative housing market is no different from the stock market. When the fictitious price of houses deviates too much from the real prices, people feel the pinch and slow down buying.

When the market becomes slow, real estate investors start selling their homes to recoup their investment and millions of homes flood the market, becoming a buyer's market. As a natural turn of events, house prices decline.

Though the housing industry has all the characteristics of a stock market, houses are not sold as frequently as stocks. While stocks are traded every day, people typically sell their homes every three to five years. This is the reason why a real estate crash will not happen in one day. The stock market can crash 20 percent or more in one day. However, real estate market crashes are slow and prolonged for years.

When house prices go down, banks worry about the loans they have made to risky buyers. When such houses go into foreclosure, banks lose substantial amounts of money. The amount lost depends on the number of risky loans they may have awarded and the size of the bubble was. Some investors take equity loans on their homes and invest in stock market or sell stocks to buy homes, depending on the market conditions. Because of this interdependency, the housing bubble and stock bubble affect each other. A housing bubble combined with a stock bubble could cause a serious economic slowdown.

EVOLUTIONARY SOLUTIONS TO THE HOUSING BUBBLE

Looking at the real estate market from an evolutionary angle, it has grown exactly as per the evolutionary principles. It has followed all three criteria of the principle of desire: Invention/Evolution (I/E), Quality, and Cost.

The primary desire that drives the real estate market is property ownership. Owning a home is everyone's dream. Real estate market evolved to satisfy buyer needs. There are more varieties now than ever before, - many price options, many locations, different sizes – homes have flooded the market. Banks offered loans to builders to build more homes as the demand grew. As many people cannot afford to pay in full, the evolution criterion "mortgage" came into existence. As the demand for mortgages increased, banks developed variations of mortgages like 30yr fixed, 15yr fixed, ARM and so on to suit the market.

Further, to satisfy the "quality" criteria, both government and banks have laid down many rules and regulations to award loans and to transfer ownership of the property to the owner. To satisfy the "cost" criteria, the banks have competed and have been offering competitive interest rates.

Applying the principle of globalization to the real estate market, as the market evolved, banks opened their doors to international investment, so individuals and businesses could invest in real estate outside of their country of residence. This has led to substantial growth in real estate investment, both in developed and developing countries.

All this looks well organized, so why then do we have housing bubbles? Real estate bubbles form whenever mortgage as a product loses its utility value. We can understand this better if we apply the first principle to the mortgage as a product.

The utility value of mortgage as a product is its profitability for the banks. Banks invest money in mortgages with the expectation they will profit from the interest earned. It follows the more money invested in mortgages, the more money they make. This is true, however, only if homebuyers have the ability to repay when the economy fluctuates. This is the reason why banks require down payments of 10 percent to 20 percent as a buffer to counter these economic fluctuations.

However, the utility value of the mortgage may not always increase by just increasing the down payment. In fact, if the banks increase the down payments beyond what the market can afford, the growth of the real estate market may even slow down. Now, the question is how to increase the utility value of mortgages while promoting a modest growth?

Although it appears that a less risky loan is the answer, it is not easy to find the risks involved. When the economy fluctuates, some people may lose jobs and some companies may go bankrupt, in turn causing the utility value of the mortgage to fluctuate. Even if the bank has verified all the documents and given out loans to less risky customers, the economic situation may change making those customers more risky. Currently borrowers are not monitored after the loan is awarded. The banks are also not assessing how risky their own investments have become until the customers begin to fall behind their payments or homes begin to foreclose. Homebuyers regularly invest money in several risky places, making it manually impossible to track them down to evaluate how risky they have become. Even if the banks appear sound, the utility value of its mortgages keeps fluctuating. For a safe and healthy economy, it all comes down to how frequently the banks reevaluate the utility of their existing mortgages.

Another aspect most banks overlook or misinterpret is the value of homes during a real estate bubble. During a bubble formation, the price of homes steadily rises increasing the equity of homes and many banks think their investments are safe or have grown. When the bubble bursts, the utility value takes a nosedive. We need to understand the importance of the utility value of the mortgages for a healthy real estate economy.

Now imagine a bank giving out loans to risky customers with very limited background check on them. When the economy slows, it should not surprise any one if these banks go bankrupt. This is exactly what happened during the real estate crash of 2006.

AUTOMATION IS THE ANSWER

Having understood the importance of utility value of mortgages, now the question is why our banks are not monitoring or managing the utility values of their investment. The truth is, banks are helpless because of lack of real-time financial data.

The consolidated financial database discussed earlier will substantially increase the utility value of mortgages. Once such a database was established, banks could launch their own loan software to track down the financial status of every borrower, be it a person or a company, to identify the risk before awarding a loan. The software will monitor factors related to the borrower such as net savings, future earnings potential, the stability of the industry employing the borrower, and so on. The more accurate the information it gathers, the more accurate the utility value of the mortgage.

Although there are many "credit reporting agencies" that can report consumers' credit histories, they do not help much to find some of the factors discussed above to evaluate the utility values of mortgages accurately. Even though some banks do make effort to have some of these features in their loan programs, today's information flow is not fast enough.

To increase the utility value even further, in the future, loan processing will be fully automated. No paperwork will be required for a decision to be made. Human involvement in making a decision on a loan makes it an inefficient process, as well as increasing chances of error, either intentional or otherwise. With automation, most bank loans will be less risky as the software programs will instantly evaluate the applicant's financial ability without subterfuge or human error.

Even after the loans are awarded, the software will continue to evaluate the mortgages' utility value based on the changing global economy and the banks can figure out how risky their loans are, well before the customers fall behind their payments. When the economy fluctuates, the software would screen out the customers that belong to the risky category. How well they identify the future risky customers depends on how extensive is the data collected from the global economy and at what speed.

More sophisticated the software become, the utility value of mortgages grow that much accurate. They will be intelligent enough to identify the bubbles forming in the real estate well in advance. The banks can put more restrictions like higher down payments in those areas where bubble is forming.

Information technology will reduce the fictitious demand for real estate caused by easy credit. With software-controlled regulation in place, many activities like sub-prime mortgages will become obsolete. With this kind of closely monitored money lending, the housing market will grow gradually and will encounter gentler price adjustments than a bubble followed by an inevitable crash.

Compare this futuristic software regulated real estate market to the current one. When prices begin to climb, all investors jump in to invest causing huge bubbles. Not only buyers suffer from losses when the bubble burst, banks are also affected hurting the economy.

The following diagram shows how the transaction information from the real world will help many agencies and individuals.

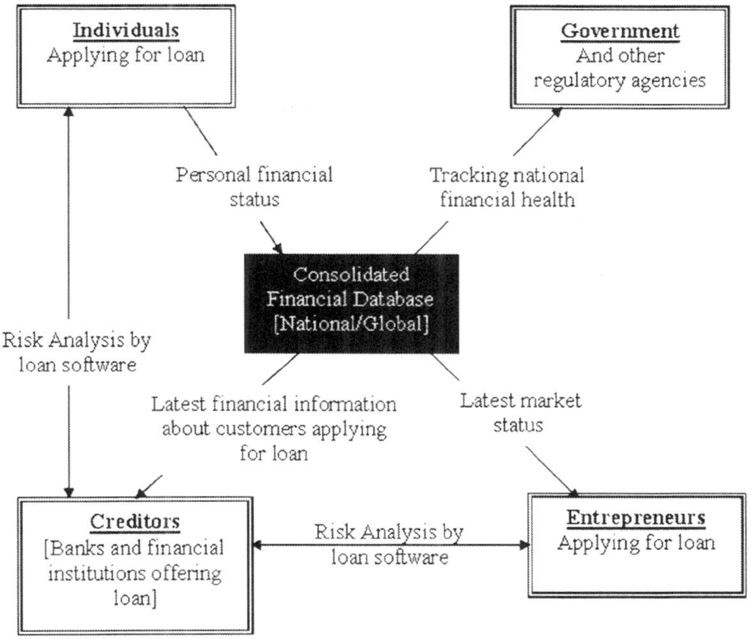

Fig 25: Using Consolidated Database to Reduce Housing Bubble

It has always been a human dream to acquire more wealth. This desire has been and will continue to be the backbone of technological evolution. However, acquiring wealth itself should not cause recession in the economy.

EFFECT OF GLOBALIZATION ON REAL ESTATE

As the global economy spreads its tentacles into all developed and underdeveloped countries, global economic activity will increase. As we know, the demand for housing depends on the economic activity. Population in cities will continue to rise to support the flourishing economy.

In the expanding global market, customers will invest locally as well as overseas where they feel there is growth potential. Don't be surprised if the owner of your neighbor's home lives in some other country, collecting rent electronically. People will buy and sell homes around the world, a trend that will predominate in the near future, as more and more underdeveloped countries prosper due to outsourcing and entry into the global market.

We will see a surge in demand for homes, by which time Information Technology will be efficient enough to filter out risky investors. Sophisticated Information Technology will regulate a fast growing global economy more efficiently than humans will today. This will promote healthy real estate growth with very little or no bubble formation.

You may already have experienced the amount of documentation needed for loan processing since the real estate market collapse. This trend for more documentation will continue in the future to avoid risky customers. As real estate businesses become more global, this paper documentation will become more of a laid-back system and becomes a bottleneck to process the loan applications more efficiently. Especially when dealing with offshore investments, more sophistication is needed than hard copies of bank statements. This automatically brings in the consolidated financial databases discussed earlier.

FUTURE OF REAL ESTATE

Let us look little deeper into the future of real estate. Information technology will begin to affect real estate market in two ways. Firstly, as we move towards the Age of Automation, the speed of transportation increases considerably with technological advancement. If you can travel 100 miles in 10 minutes, do you really care about your daily commute? We will be less concerned about the traffic congestion and the commuting stress, which affects the price of real estate to a significant level.

Secondly, with high-speed computer networks, future employees will work from home eliminating the need to travel long distances. In essence, home location becomes inconsequential.

With more automation, homebuyers aspire to have more comforts and luxuries in their homes. In future homes, location becomes less significant and the hi-tech features the house has to offer become more important.

As home building technology keeps growing, we will see new homes being built in a matter of days rather than months or years. With sophisticated machines, we will see new towns and cities built in remote locations with RAP machines.

When automation sets in, the demand for housing will be immediately met by machines without multiple people bidding for the same house. Home prices drop to the actual construction value without any effect of "location value." Just like any other manufacturing product, the house prices will follow the quality-ladder that we discussed earlier. Future homes will not only be highly affordable, but will be recycled often and climb the evolutionary ladder.

CHAPTER 15

EVOLUTIONARY SOLUTION TO EXPENSIVE EDUCATION

Though our world is growing at an unprecedented pace, higher education is still a dream for many. Colleges are so expensive many families cannot afford it. Data from The National Center for Public Policy and Higher Education shows the increasing cost of education. The increase in the price of college has outstripped price increases in other sectors of the economy.

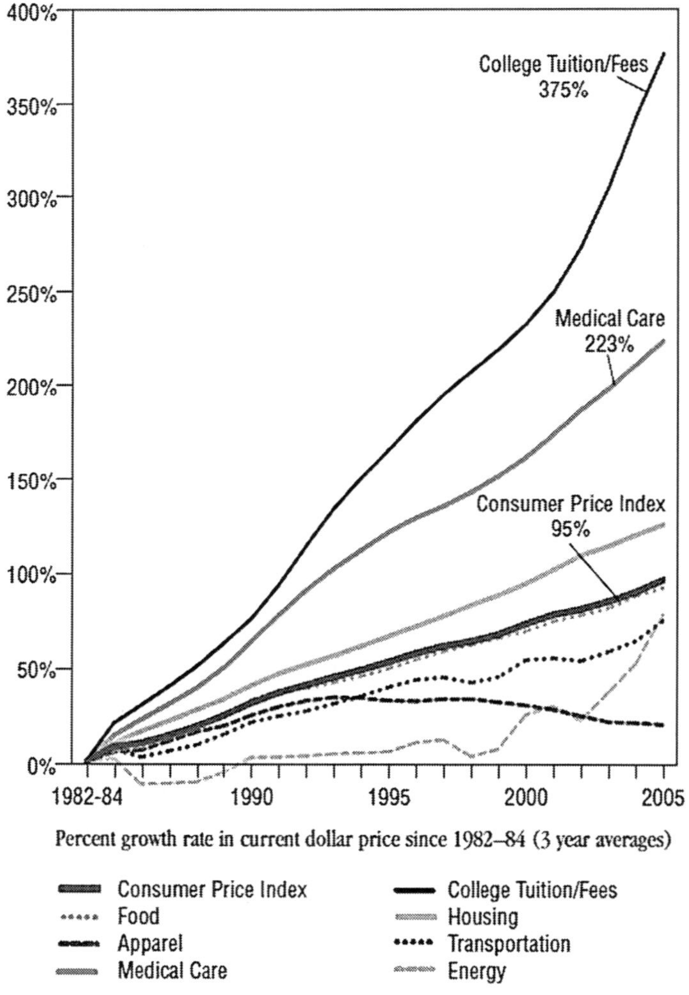

Fig 26: Increase in the price of college and other sectors of the economy.
Source: The National Center for Public Policy and Higher Education
Percent growth rates calculated based on Consumer Price Index for All Urban Consumers, available at the Bureau of Labor Statistics website, http://stats.bls.gov/. All industries above are components of the CPI. College Tuition/Fees represent sticker price tuition and fees less all types of grant aid except grants

related to athletics and other student talents for undergraduate and graduate studies at 2-year or 4-year colleges, major universities, and professional schools. Room and board charges and textbook charges are not included. Data were collected from 88 metropolitan cities. Food & Beverage includes food at home; food away from home, and alcoholic beverages. Housing includes rent of primary residence, lodging away from home, owners' equivalent rent of primary residence, and tenants' and household insurance. (Only the "shelter" category was used in this analysis.) Apparel includes men's and boys' apparel, women's and girls' apparel, infants' and toddlers' apparel, and footwear. Transportation includes private transportation (new and used motor vehicles, fuel, parts and equipment, maintenance and repair) and public transportation. Medical Care includes medical care commodities (prescription drugs, over-the-counter-drugs, and other medical equipment and supplies) and medical care services (professional medical services, hospital or nursing home services, and health insurance imputation). Energy includes fuel oil, other household fuels, electricity, utility natural gas services, and motor fuel.

By entering the work force after completing school or dropping out of school, many young people start making money early on in their lives. They can exercise their own independence and support their family at the same time. Only some can afford to attend college. Unfortunately, this kind of education for the rich only is slowing our evolutionary pace.

In October 2008, only 68.6 percent of high school graduates were enrolled in colleges or universities, according to data released by the Bureau of Labor Statistics of the United States Department of Labor. Of these, nearly 19 percent dropped out before completing college. Financial difficulty is found to be the primary reason for college dropouts.

We lose contributions from many bright students, as they do not attend colleges where they can utilize their innate intelligence; instead, they use their muscles to work in entry-level jobs fresh out of high school. We are concerned about these dropouts and students who cannot afford college because they matter to our ultimate evolution as a planet and, therefore, as a species. A less educated nation contributes more slowly to human technological evolution, while a highly educated nation contributes significantly.

Three factors are responsible for the rising cost of today's education system.

1. **Capital Investment:** We want the best of everything – the best laboratories, the best sports facilities, great campuses, and the list is endless. Colleges have invested and will continue to invest heavily in all infrastructures that make education more costly. This high cost is born out of our own desire for more.

2. **Faculty:** Nearly two-thirds of education cost is attributed to faculty salary. Good teachers cost more. To stay competitive, colleges have to employ the best.

3. **Productivity:** Any college or university that tries to enroll more students per class to increase productivity will face a negative effect. Students need lower student-to-teacher ratio.

Looking at these factors responsible for the cost of education, it appears as though the cost will continue to rise, as there is no reason for it to decrease.

THE EVOLUTIONARY APPROACH

Our schools and colleges have evolved and will continue to evolve to satisfy the human desire for better education. In today's environment, without good colleges, a nation cannot progress. We are seeing this in the world of outsourcing. Jobs are going to countries where education and training systems are well established and abundant young graduates are available.

Although these colleges are contributing substantially to overall economic growth, they are also evolving just like any other industry. The irony is their growth itself has made education very expensive. Competitive colleges are constantly adding infrastructure, making the education more expensive. This education cost is going to skyrocket as technology progresses.

Now let us look at this problem from an evolutionary angle. From the principle of globalization, we know any product or service will become affordable and evolve into the future at a much faster pace if it goes global. Our colleges are no different.

The good news is there is no need to globalize our colleges from scratch. Many colleges are already online, offering courses that do not require students to attend a campus, nor stay on campus in student housing. However, the drawback to online learning is some courses are not considered equal to classroom learning, because students do not have the opportunity to participate in face-to-face discussions and lack hands on experience.

This limitation has not deflated online education. Many students take online education for various reasons – enhancing their career path, promotion, higher salaries, and sometimes just to enhance their knowledge. Existing online education will evolve as discussed below.

COMPETITION IN TEACHING

Good teachers are in all institutions and not limited to any one particular college or university. Students will greatly benefit from these great teachers' classroom lessons available online. This applies to both regular full time and online students. Good teachers are not hard to find in colleges. While students flock to popular classes, some classes are scarcely attended. By putting the classes taught by good teachers online, colleges benefit all students globally. Their very online presence will make a difference to education system. Students may attend these online classes to **supplement** their regular course **for a nominal fee**. If a teacher in a particular subject is not good enough, the student can supplement it via online classes taught by popular teachers. This will bring more revenue to popular online teachers and motivate them to teach even better. As a first step towards globalization of education, colleges and universities must allow their classes to be supplemented with online classes. In addition, gradually they should open their doors to the world that will substantially increase the quality of education.

The other amazing influence of online classes is their availability. In traditional classes, students cannot go back to earlier classes or fast forward to later classes, as they are scheduled successively. Many colleges are already allowing students to record classroom discussions to circumvent these problems. The archive of online classes will boost their availability as classes could be taken any time during the day or night.

Once these online classes are available, an obvious thing that happens to the education system is it becomes very affordable. Colleges and universities are now depending on limited revenue from fulltime students and some financial assistance from governments. When they open their doors to the global market the revenue will be substantial. For example, if a teacher has enrolled one million online students, at a fee of say one dollar per class (this is a random number, although monthly or annual memberships are possible), the income is one million dollars per class. With that kind of money, our modern system of education will become a truly successful global business, as it should evolve to be. With this high revenue, there will be an unprecedented demand for good teachers. Becoming an online professor will soon be a very high paying profession.

Although online education will attract students globally, online students will still be lagging behind in the hands-on experience students receive in a classroom environment. Colleges will have to evolve technologically to cater to those students.

AUTOMATION IN EDUCATION

A great new development we will see in the near future in the education industry is the extensive use of virtual reality education (VR-ed) devices that will offer students the same experience as that of regular classroom students. Existing virtual reality devices will become more sophisticated. These devices will not only be exposed to the global market but also come under intense pressure to evolve to provide the needed interaction between student, teacher and the classroom environment. These devices will make the classroom experience very effective for online students.

WHAT ABOUT NOT-SO-GOOD TEACHERS?

Would this system become a threat to not-so-good teachers? Would they lose their jobs if they did not perform to modern standards? Those who are interested in education career but not good in teaching can help online teachers by doing needed research work for them. As the market grows, there will also be more demand for research associates in the future. Successful online teachers will need a good research group to find the latest information to deliver quality lectures and to set up highly interactive classrooms and laboratories. The technology also keeps evolving at a much faster pace. As a result, the future of classrooms and laboratories will be vastly advanced. Millions of dollars will go into making this possible. The real teachers will constantly need up-to-date research and training to stay current in the competitive global market. In fact, research in preparation to deliver quality education online will grow as a global industry. As universities cater to the entire world, their capability, infrastructure, and revenue all will grow along the evolutionary path.

By applying the principles of evolution, we have learned technology is the main culprit for increased educational cost. Be it a state-of-the-art laboratory or sports facility, the cost raises as technology improves. By globalizing the educational system, colleges increase the market size and earn more revenue, bringing down the cost of education and making global education possible.

Even though there is a huge market for education, colleges and universities have not yet opened their doors to the outside world. By bringing their classrooms to the global market, developed countries will not only evolve faster, but give an opportunity for underdeveloped countries to grow as well.

With the potential online revenue at stake, colleges will compete to offer the best education online. Future online colleges will establish their own research departments to make available the latest and the greatest information to students. The laboratory demonstrations will use hi-tech gadgets. Students will learn much faster by attending these competing online colleges around the world. This is possible because of intense competition among both colleges and students to succeed in a competitive world. While students look for the best online classes, colleges look for the best teachers to stay competitive. Imagine the effect of such high quality and low cost education on the world's technological evolution.

EDUCATION IN UNDERDEVELOPED NATIONS

Now let us take a step back to our current world scenario. In today's underdeveloped countries, many villages have no schools at all. Even if they had schools, local people cannot afford to send their children to schools. In those poor villages, children are expected to earn money for the family rather than attend school. In some countries this is strictly illegal, while in others it is a way of life. Catching perpetrators is extremely difficult, especially in countries where the majority of the population is poor.

In war torn countries, where the economy is in shambles and poverty is at its peak, businesses are shuttered and unemployment rampant. Schools have been closed indefinitely. Children have no place to go except the streets, where they indulge in activities that may be counterproductive to themselves and society in general.

In such places, education for children and money for families is the starting point to initiate development in those countries. A paid-to-attend kind of education system is often the only hope in such places. Students not only get free education, their families are paid for their children's regular attendance. Private organizations should consider investing in these educational industries. In return for the investment, students work for those organizations after graduation for a predetermined period so the companies gain some profit from their investment.

With low cost, online education as discussed above, education is very affordable even for private companies to make an investment. With paid education, we will see a dramatic improvement in those communities. Paid education will not only be a great tool to control crime, it will increase the morale and standard of living as well. Once the families are paid to lead a hunger-free life and children are educated for free, their focus will change from daily survival to their future advancement. They will begin to look at a new future for themselves and future generations.

Though these private companies will take risks initially, they will soon reap the benefits. With such a huge number of new global employees, combined with plenty of global jobs from an exploding global economy, we will see a more productive world. These once-depressed regions will contribute to the global economy. This approach will transform these countries into advanced nations.

By indoctrinating an entire generation of people to think of education as an industry rather than as a luxury for the chosen few, technological evolution will be that much easier for them – and future generations as well.

CHAPTER 16

EVOLUTIONARY ANGLE TO THE OUTSOURCING CRISIS

Outsourcing has become a most controversial issue and highly debated subject in the world today. In this chapter, we will look at outsourcing from an evolutionary angle and analyze if this is really taking us in the right direction.

Two major categories of jobs that are getting outsourced are blue-collar and white-collar jobs. The outsourced blue-collar jobs include all manufacturing jobs. The outsourced white-collar jobs include all skilled jobs related to Information Technology, telecommunication, biotechnology research, financial analysts, architectural drafters, telemarketers, accountants, medical billing, medical transcriptions, claims adjusters, home loan processors and so on. The list of jobs keeps changing as the factors responsible for outsourcing changes.

There are three factors responsible for outsourcing – labor **C**ost, skill **A**vailability, and the **S**peed of Information Technology (CAS for short). Each one of these CAS factors will boost the pace of outsourcing and also continually transform the outsourcing market. If a country offers skilled, low cost labor and Information Technology is sophisticated enough for fast communication, then outsourcing happens seamlessly.

Let us discuss both blue and while-collar categories and examine their affect on our economy.

EFFECT OF BLUE-COLLAR OUTSOURCING

Blue-collar outsourcing has both positive and negative effects on our economy. Let us look at an example and see how it affects the local businesses. Say a private company manufacturing shoes with local workers sells a shoe for $50. If that company outsourced its jobs to another country, the cost of a shoe might be cut to $20 or less.

The negative impact is partial or complete layoffs depending on the extent of the outsourcing. The price reduction will put pressure on other shoe manufacturers to outsource their jobs as well, increasing the number of layoffs. The employees who lost their jobs will need to be retrained to be able to join the work force, either in the same company at a different level or in a different company altogether. They will have an opportunity to change their career, if they were able to adapt. If the laid off employees were older, then the transition will be more difficult.

The positive impact of outsourcing is the increased market size because of the price reduction. Even poor people will be able to afford shoes at this price level. More sales mean more economic activity.

This impact is from just one product. As more and more low cost products come into the market, the market size will expand, and the transportation industry will become busier. The international shipping industry will become busy and the domestic transportation system will improve. These expanded industries will hire more workers. Increased sales will bring more shopping malls and expand existing malls, offering construction and maintenance jobs to many workers. The expanded shopping complexes will hire sales employees and support other services like food courts, creating a ripple effect in other business sectors.

Increased sales will affect the credit card industry as well, with more transactions and as a result, more revenue. This industry will hire more people as their operations expanded. Banks will open more ATM machines, as the need for cash to make purchases increases. Banks will hire employees for various operations.

This seemingly small act of reducing the price of goods and services will have endless ramifications for every other tentacle of the marketplace. So simply to say, "No," to outsourcing is to blindly stem the tide of industry growth. A few jobs lost in one sector might lead to more—and better—jobs in another sector.

Every other industry will benefit to some extent by a reduction in prices and increased sales. Price reductions help poor people, too, as even they begin to shop as a result of their improved standard of living.

Reduction in price does not mean people will buy more, but it means more people will be able to afford those products and services. We would see a bigger crowd in the shopping malls.

Regular buyers may not spend more but may buy more for the same price. For the same weekly or monthly fixed budget, they will take home more products than before. However, what we should notice is the market size will be much greater than when prices were high which means the revenue earned by the companies will be substantially higher. Governments will collect more tax revenue and be able to offer a better infrastructure to its citizens.

Lower prices substantially increase the living standard of people. For example, shoppers who used to buy two pair of shoes for $100 will now buy five pairs or more on the same $100 budget. For arguments sake, instead of buying one hundred products for $1,000, shoppers will be able to buy three hundred to four hundred products for the same amount. This increases their standard of living substantially. Again, it is not just products but also an entire ripple effect that will branch out across multiple industries and income streams. In fact, this is equivalent to seeing three hundred to four hundred shops open in place of one hundred shops, leading to more activity in all other services discussed above. We may lose some jobs during outsourcing, however, once prices fall, every other local industry will expand and hire more employees. In effect, outsourcing produces more jobs locally than otherwise.

This is just one side of the coin. When market size increases, global businesses have to produce more. Higher mass production leads to further reduction in price. The price falls until it reaches the lowest the outsourced country can afford to offer. The competition to capture a bigger market by price reduction forces businesses to look for low cost labor in other countries as well. The search for low cost labor is an ongoing battle critical to the success of business. Every time the prices fall, the local economy grows that much bigger. The local market benefits from these outsourcing efforts.

When underdeveloped countries are transformed into developing countries, they in turn became customers in the global market. Their increased standard of living and market size affects many other countries around the world, increasing the global market's overall size.

Imagine the impact of more countries developing. What will be the size of that global economy? Global industries will be very busy to cater to such a demand. Looking beyond outsourcing and into future effects of outsourcing, we see amazing growth and a world full of opportunities.

The following diagram shows the ripple effects of outsourcing blue-collar jobs.

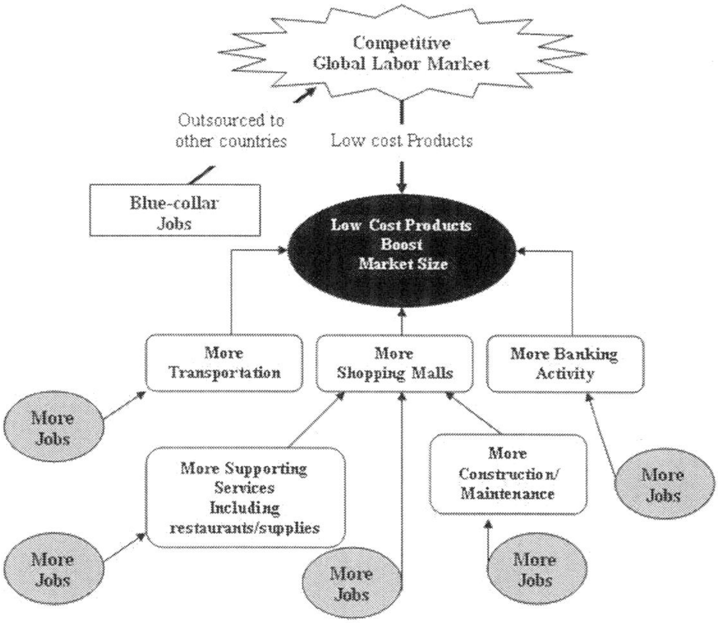

Fig 27: Effects of Blue-Collar Outsourcing

Today, outsourcing has become so common new companies consider outsourcing from day one. Part of their organizational blueprint includes the costs – and savings – of outsourcing key positions, particularly blue-collar labor. Businesses may not even open their fabrication units in developed countries. The good news is nearly 70 percent of the jobs are hard to outsource and they fall under "local service jobs" category. Only 30 percent of the jobs have the potential to get outsourced.

EFFECT OF WHITE-COLLAR JOB OUTSOURCING

Over the past few years, skilled labor has also been outsourced. Some research skills, which require PhD degrees, are so rare even in developed countries it is necessary to outsource them to other developing countries for faster research and development.

Other skills, including Information Technology, that do not need doctoral degrees, are outsourced for both skill and cost reasons. These jobs are moving from country to country depending on low cost and skill availability.

None of these skilled jobs has any national borders. In this digital age, the employee can be in any country and join the work force. With such global availability of labor and easy access via computer networks, it is relatively easy to set up a global organization. The headquarters can be in one country and its branches spread to several other countries. This kind of organizational structure brings in the best available skill at a low cost and helps grow the global market even larger.

The diagram below shows mutual outsourcing of white-collar jobs

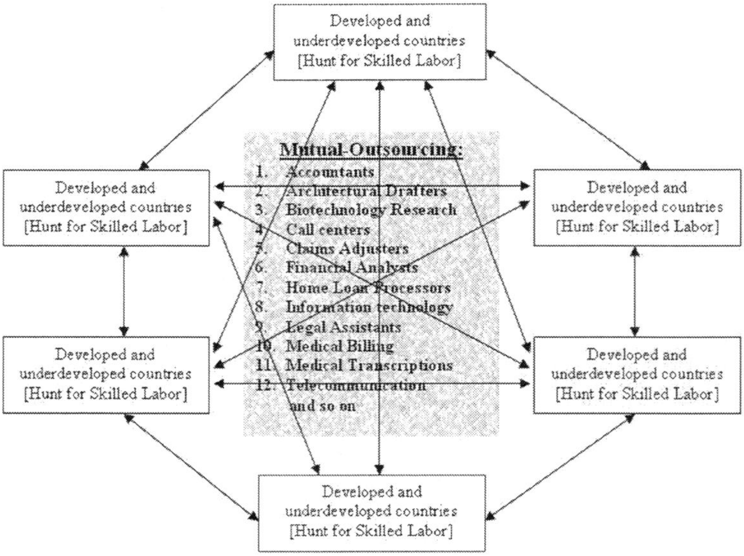

Fig 28: Mutual Outsourcing

We get a much better understanding of these white-collar jobs looking at the outsourcing from the evolutionary point of view. Consider the example of Information Technology (IT) outsourcing. It appears to threaten local job markets in developed countries. However, the reality is much different.

When IT jobs are outsourced, the company's capability increases. It can produce more and better software for the same investment. For instance, in place of one video game, the company now can produce three or four games for the same cost. This is because, the company can hire as many as four to five employees for the salary of one that is paid in a developed country like the United States or Europe. Instead of one version of software produced every two years, the outsourcing company may produce a new version every three months. A GPS may get updated maps every month instead of once every year or two.

More products fetch more revenue for the company and as costs come down, market size increases. To satisfy bigger markets, production has to go up making the company hire more employees overseas. More employees are also needed locally to manage the outsourced projects. This is how the positive feedback loop begins to take effect in all outsourced businesses.

Other competing companies outsource, too, and their capability increases. Because of increased market size, many new companies emerge and we see more employment opportunities both in overseas and local markets. A company producing ten software products a year with ten employees before outsourcing, could now produce fifty software products or more with the capabilities of outsourcing. As the market size increases, they now need more than ten employees locally and several hundred people overseas. This positive feedback loop keeps creating more jobs both locally and overseas. The number of jobs created locally will soon exceed the jobs lost. While this is just one side of the effect, there could be ripple effects on other industries.

With more jobs outsourced, there will be a tremendous need for infrastructure and networking in outsourced countries. With millions of people needing access via the network, the telecommunication and networking industries in developed countries will get a boost as they expand their capacity and hire local people to expand the telecommunication networks.

What is the impact on international shipping and travel? The ships and airlines will get their share as more goods are transported and more people travel all over the world for business meetings, sales/marketing, contract jobs, and so on. We see job opportunities here too. What is the impact on international banking? With so many transactions going on in the world, the banks will need more people. Growth of just one industry will have a substantial effect on other dependent industries. **It is sad we are not able to relate these developments to outsourcing.**

If we look back and see how we evolved all these centuries, these kinds of developments take time. However, with outsourcing, the pace is so high that we are seeing all these effects in our lifetime.

Let us examine the effect of the positive feedback loop on the global economy. As underdeveloped countries develop, there will be more demand for education and training. The online education system that we discussed earlier will get a boost to support such a huge global demand and there will be availability of more skilled labor. In the future, as underdeveloped countries advance, it will be hard to say which country is outsourcing to which. The skill level being outsourced eventually will become "mutual outsourcing" spread all over the world.

World keep growing continuously and the demand for skilled labor never slow down until we feel that the 6.5 billion people are not big enough and we need more people! When we look at the outsourcing crisis from evolutionary eyes, we see the future world as a network of intellectual humans commanding a host of machines that do all but the manual jobs. Outsourcing is just the beginning of that massive development.

RAG TO RICHES

Have you heard of a rag to riches story and wondered how fortunate those people have been? In an evolutionary world, these will not be just stories but will happen in everyone's lives.

In an underdeveloped country, where you see someone carrying weight on their head or pulling a cart to make a living or lying down on the street out of sheer hunger, our evolutionary eyes should see it in a different perspective. Billions of poor people live in slums and poor towns. Our eyes should see nothing but opportunities for world prosperity at an amazing speed. We should imagine training and job opportunities knocking on their doors. We should imagine filthy towns transforming into advanced worlds. Though our current economy is not growing fast enough to capture the intellectual ability of these people, though it takes time to train these illiterate people to make them intellectual contributors to society, the positive feedback loop of globalization will eventually make it happen. Online education will soon reach every nook and cranny of the world.

How quickly rags could turn to riches depends on how quickly our global economy expands. Our evolutionary eyes should find ways to increase this pace of economic growth with no bubbles.

CHAPTER 17

PLANNING YOUR CAREER

Planning a career is the hardest decision one can make, especially when many jobs are being outsourced. In planning your career, choosing a job that does not have the potential to be outsourced is as important as understanding the evolutionary phases of your job so you will not be laid off as the world progresses.

As discussed earlier, outsourcing happens to cut costs. In this era of globalization, no job is safe in either developed or developing countries. Even in fast growing countries like China and India, the jobs have the potential to be outsourced to other low cost countries. If the businesses find another country where the labor cost is low, jobs are re-outsourced to those places. The good news about outsourcing is it creates more local service jobs that are difficult to outsource.

To understand the job market, let us create three categories: jobs that are currently being outsourced, jobs that are hard to outsource, and jobs that have the potential to grow without being outsourced.

CURRENTLY OUTSOURCED JOBS

Software programming, medical bill processing, medical transcription, accounting, call center and technical support, data entry, paralegal, tax preparation, biomedical research and so on.

Note: As this list changes from time to time, further research will be needed for the latest information.

If you find your job among these, it does not mean you cannot find jobs in these areas. It only means they are good targets for outsourcing, as they do not require an employee's physical presence to deliver the customer service. Any job that does not strictly require physical presence to interact with the customer has the potential to get outsourced. As Information Technology improves, more jobs fall into this category.

JOBS THAT ARE HARD TO OUTSOURCE

Physicians, Lawyers, Physicians Assistant, Dental Assistant, Physical therapy, Pharmacist, School/College Teachers, Fitness trainer, Sports coaches and so on.

Note: Again, as this list changes from time to time, further research will be needed for the latest information.

These professions need a physical presence to serve their customers and have very little potential to get outsourced. Again, this does not mean they will not be outsourced at all. As automation becomes more sophisticated, partial outsourcing here, too, is possible. These professions are under the microscope like any other and businesses are searching for ways to cut costs.

Healthcare, for example, is becoming very expensive. Health insurance companies will find ways to automate many processes to reduce cost. If you are planning entry into the healthcare profession, you need to evaluate your skill and ability to face the challenges when it is automated in the future. We are already seeing the impact of automation in healthcare, driving doctors to learn additional technical skills every year to remain competitive. The number of diagnostic devices increases each year. Many new technologies for medical procedures are emerging onto the market. Documentation is becoming electronic. Accessing patient medical information via online has become fairly common in many developed countries. If you look at this profession from an evolutionary angle, it has all the characteristics of being heavily automated in the near future.

As healthcare costs climb due to technology, cost reduction will become the focus for the health insurance companies. Treating a sick patient is very expensive. Treating the same problem at an early stage is highly cost effective. Preventing the same ailment is much cheaper. The earlier symptoms are diagnosed, the more money the company saves. You will see a host of health monitoring devices in the future that collect and send patient data routinely.

Online diagnosis and remote patient monitoring will become the business model for the healthcare industry in the future. Availability of automated software and machines will increase to meet the demand. Healthcare professionals must keep learning these new technologies. No longer is it just healthcare knowledge that will suffice for doctors and other healthcare professionals in the future, but they will have to face the challenges of automation.

Teaching jobs will face similar competition when they go online. Online colleges will increase in number in the near future. If you are planning to be in this profession, be prepared to meet the competition to become a successful online teacher or be prepared to be a research associate to support online teachers, which needs continuous research to get the latest and greatest information to compete with other online institutions.

The bottom line is, in the future, these professions, though they are hard to outsource, continually require hi-tech knowledge as they are automated. For any of these professions, you will need an aptitude to adapt to ever changing automation to be successful.

JOBS THAT HAVE THE POTENTIAL TO GROW

Plumbing, Electrician, Auto repair, Home construction, Mail/Courier service, Restaurant jobs, Security, Banking and so on.

Note: Again, as this list changes from time to time, further research will be needed for the latest information.

Just like the previous category of jobs, these jobs also require physical presence to serve their customers and have very low potential to get outsourced. At the same time, they have the potential to grow and expand because of globalization. You may heave a sigh of relief at finding jobs that will expand in the future instead of collapsing like others. However, there is a catch. As these jobs cannot be outsourced, their demand increases when the globalization pace increases. As a result, skilled workers become harder to find, making them expensive. Plumbing, electrical, construction and a host of other service jobs become expensive as rapidly as globalization spreads. These jobs suddenly look very lucrative. Many people may even change careers to get into these high paying jobs. The question is, "will they remain lucrative?"

Globalization is, after all, a process of reducing cost. If the cost of labor increases in any profession, automation will find an evolutionary solution for it.

When a service becomes expensive, as a natural turn of events, many businesses develop alternative automation ideas. For example, new houses and commercial buildings will incorporate automation ideas that require less maintenance. For example, we will see new designs of HVAC systems and home appliances that will have fail-over systems. Many of these appliances may have two or three parallel electronic circuits to avoid instant failure. Only one will be in working mode while others will be in standby mode. With this kind of failsafe system, less maintenance and less frequent repairs will be needed. They may cost a little more initially, but with mass production, they will eventually become cheaper.

When appliances finally break down, customers will get a remote diagnosis of their appliance to figure out what is needed before dispatching a service person. Currently, when an appliance breaks down, a service person living miles away comes to your home only to find it needs a small fuse replacement. However, you are charged by the hour as they have lost time, too.

Further, appliance services can be done remotely if they are designed with that capability. We have already seen remote repair of computers, modems and a host of digital devices. This creates a demand for smart appliances that can be remotely diagnosed and serviced, lowering the overall cost. This brings us to the doorstep of automation.

You may have already seen that kind of automation in energy meter reading and water meter reading. The new machines installed in your home gives out digital information and the meter reader driving in front of your home gets the reading as they drives, with no need to stop to check the meter. What a cost saver.

We may soon see home appliances that can be installed from outside. This assists service people to replace it without requiring your presence. This means they can quickly plug it in and move on. In today's world, installation is a very time consuming process. Service people set up an appointment with you and arrange to get access to your home. Each house configuration and installation is different, adding to the installation time. With this plug and play method, they can service many homes at the same time. If there is traffic congestion, they can even service at night, saving even more time.

In fact, in the future, as the home appliances are remotely monitored, the service people will know when they break down, even before you know it. They will be repaired or replaced while you are at work. Those days are not far off, as the technology is already available.

Low maintenance homes with "plug from outside" appliances will make the once lucrative service jobs more competitive. Remote monitoring, remote maintenance of advanced home appliances will become a challenge for service personnel in the future. If you look at these safe jobs of today from an evolutionary angle, they are great candidates for automation. If you are planning your career around these service jobs, plan on living with these automations.

The same logical explanation goes with automobile repair. Services become much more expensive as the technology of cars advances. Most cars will be diagnosed remotely to reduce costs. We already see remote monitoring technology developing in many cars. Technology for unlocking cars remotely is common. The oil change we do regularly may become very rare in the near future. Soon you will find maintenance free cars that do not require any regular maintenance and the customers need not have to drive to the service station every 3 months. These cars will be remotely diagnosed for problems and remotely monitored, to check the car's health. If there is any potential problem, the system will know in advance and the customer will be contacted to have it fixed. The maintenance and repair jobs will become technology intensive.

THE RULE OF THUMB

To summarize, when it comes to picking the right career, look at it from both globalization and automation point of view. The rule of thumb is, globalization will outsource jobs that do not require physical presence to serve the customer. Automation makes jobs that are hard to outsource, technologically challenging. Which means jobs will either get outsourced or will become technology intensive to move towards automation.

The bottom line is, no matter which safe career you chose, it would eventually be impacted by automation. Irrespective of the profession you choose, a good understanding of Information Technology goes a long way in helping you to adapt to changes. ***Information Technology is the language of Automation***. Learning the language of Automation at the beginning of your career will help you understand the automation better and keep you competitive throughout your career.

CHAPTER 18

EVOLUTIONARY FACE OF GREEN TECHNOLOGY

Green technology has become very popular terminology. Out of sheer concern for our planet, we have welcomed this technology into our lives, even though there is very little or no economic gain.

Although we all have to embrace this technology, all green technologies are not necessarily fully green. We need to find out how much "green" the technology is even before considering using it. For instance, even though electric cars are greener than their gasoline counterparts are, they are not fully green as the company that manufactures the battery may emit greenhouse gases. The same argument goes with organic products. Organic crops use less or no pesticides and are very healthy. However, because they use little or no pesticides, the result is a low yield crop with high cost. To increase the yield, we need more land which results in more deforestation and more machines to grow the crop. Although organic crops are healthier and greener than their non-organic counterparts are, they are not fully green. Does it mean companies are simply labeling some technologies as green even though they are not fully green? How green should a technology be for humans to consider it seriously?

A true "green" technology is one that has no impact on our ecosystem either at the manufacturing level or at the usage level. On the other hand, a "greener" technology is one that has lesser impact on our ecosystem compared to its non-green counterpart. We do not have true green technologies yet. Most of the green technologies we see around are only "greener technologies." It is the green industries' responsibility to provide data proving how green they are.

Now let us look at green technology from an evolutionary angle. There is a lot more meaning to green technology than what people generally understand.

Life on this planet is so dependent on the ecosystem that without it we cannot survive. Our planet cleans the air we breathe, the water we use, digests all the garbage we discard, and supports flora and fauna on which we depend. This dependency is not easy to break. It is like cutting the umbilical cord from Mother Nature. To break this cord, we need to develop a highly sophisticated technology that can mimic the ecosystem. This is what "green technology" is all about.

All human space voyages, including lunar landings, are examples of man's quest to explore the universe by breaking the dependency on earth's ecosystem, however short the duration may be. It is like a baby walking away from its mother and coming back after a few little baby steps – a few more steps, and then some more....

We are in that stage now, craving independence and not afraid to stray too far from Mother Nature, but cautious enough that we are not quite ready to break ties completely. Every rocket tried to mimic our ecosystem for a short period of time. That same technology will grow and improve over time, making us better able to move away from Mother Earth.

When we attempt to break this umbilical cord, one of the most important technologies that will come to our rescue is **"green technology."** When we create our own artificial atmospheres, our industries have to be fully emission free. In the future, we will be utilizing all the green technology we are developing today to keep this artificial atmosphere clean.

In fact, green technology will be so vital in these artificial atmospheres that without it we can't possibly survive. For instance, if there is carbon dioxide emission from a car, Mother Nature absorbs it. In an artificial atmosphere, it will be catastrophic. The green technology we are developing today is one of the greatest contributions we can give to our future generations.

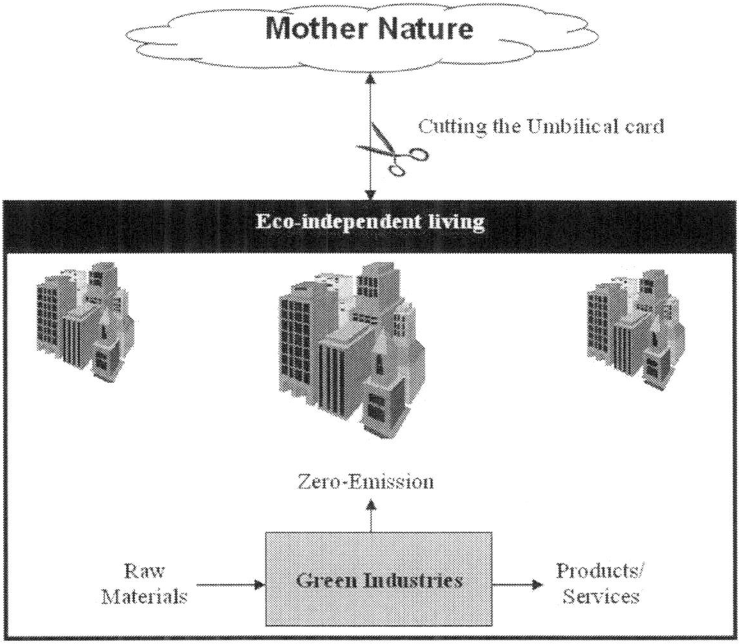

Fig 29: Eco-Independent Living in the Future

If our current global warming phenomenon had not been observed and had we not developed green technology, we probably would have developed it regardless when we tried to break away from Mother Earth. Now, thanks to global warming, we are forced to develop this technology and are better prepared to break that umbilical cord. Green technology will help us to evolve from an eco-friendly world to an eco-free world.

FOOD DOMES

As our climate is slowly but permanently changing, it is becoming harder for farmers to depend on seasonal rain. Rain may arrive early, late, or not come at all. These changes are expected to become more severe in the near future as we move into the advanced global warming phases. For continued economic growth and technological evolution, it will become exceedingly important to move away from eco dependency.

Serious research is needed to design and build artificial biospheres that can grow crops by recycling water. Instead of irrigating in open fields, crops can be grown in huge glass domes; the water evaporated from plants could be trapped and recycled. As technology improves and RAP becomes a practical reality, this design will become more sophisticated and economically viable as a stand-alone entity that could survive without any dependency on the ecosystem.

These domes will not only solve current food and water shortage problems in the world, but will dramatically transform our future food industry. As we break the umbilical cord with Mother Nature and start living in artificial atmospheres, food domes will be the only option for our food requirements. Once these domes are automated with robots, the food supply will be very dependable and not reliant on outside weather conditions.

Governments and private enterprises must promote research on these artificial biospheres at a much larger scale than is done today; as research is a time consuming process, the earlier we start, the earlier we see results.

CHAPTER 19

PRACTICING THE ART

Although we are able look at the future by using the five principles of evolution, we invariably come across many bottlenecks, which tend to slow down the evolutionary pace. When we analyze each of these bottlenecks from an evolutionary angle, they offer many workable solutions. We have so far identified the following five solutions.

Information Technology to avoid bubbles forming in our economy

RAP to produce cheap green energy and raw materials

Online diagnosis to offer high quality healthcare to the entire world

Online education to offer affordable, quality education to the entire world

Food domes to help us cut the umbilical cord with Mother Nature

The above **IROOF** solutions are born out of our own desire for a better living. These solutions will accelerate our evolutionary pace substantially, if we can address the underlying critical issues. Each one of these solutions will move us toward the Age of Automation at a faster pace.

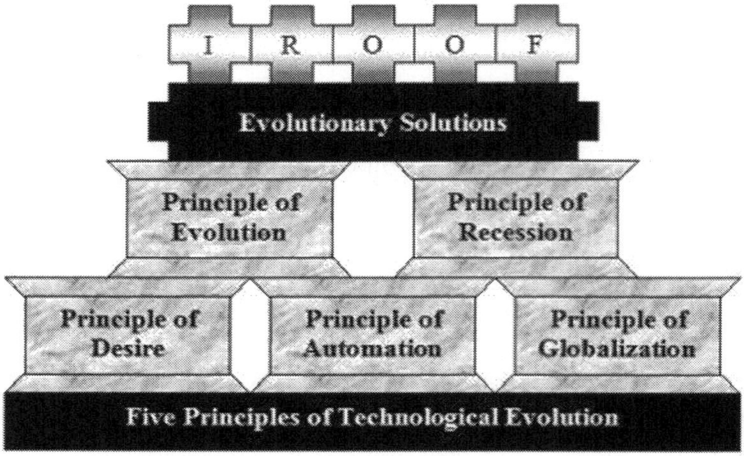

Each of the IROOF solutions has their own evolutionary effect on our slowly evolving planet.

Information technology (IT) that came into existence a few decades ago to ease our lives has become a necessity. The financial databases in today's market will continue to evolve into consolidated global databases, capturing real-time financial data from around the world. Our own desire for in-depth data and a faster information flow makes this happen. As and when paper currencies disappear from the market, the data capture becomes more efficient. **IT** becomes a lethal force against corruption and illegal trades, and will eventually establish itself as a reliable regulatory tool. With high precision data flowing around the world, tracked by sophisticated software, all of the economic bubbles will slowly fade out.

With the formation of a stock cloud in the future, the efficiency of investment will be very high. Every penny earned will flow back into the economy in the same nanosecond it was earned. With that amount of money in the stock cloud, our global industries will grow at an unprecedented pace with our standard of living growing equally well.

RAP is a natural evolution of machines to help fragile human beings achieve their evolutionary dreams. Without RAP, we will grow very slowly for an extended period, putting our evolution on "slow pace." **RAP** is very powerful when it comes to energy production, since cheap energy affects every other sector around the world. However, our real economy might get a jolt if energy became exceedingly cheap. With billions of eager consumers ready to buy cheap products, our high-paced economy will experience a roller coaster ride with bubbles forming in all sectors. Without sophisticated Information Technology, it will become humanly impossible to track down and regulate the fluctuations in our economy. Information technology should always be a step ahead of us, to guide us in the right direction. **RAP** and **IT**, if went together, will take our technological evolution in the right direction and at the right pace.

Online medical records already taking shape, "online diagnosis" is right around the corner. As technology grows to satisfy our desires, the cost of healthcare will be unaffordable to the majority of people in the very near future. When online diagnoses become a reality, the insurance companies and governments that offer healthcare will embrace it. With **RAP** and **IT** healthcare will become very affordable and the healthcare will continue to evolve the way it should be.

Online learning is the long awaited phase of our education system, which will be fast to react to the increased demands of the future. It takes years to establish traditional colleges. Online education is a natural growth of an education system to train individuals around the world to meet specific demands. Although many online colleges are already available, the real demand will come in the future in both developed and developing countries as globalization expands. Virtual reality will join hands with online education to evolve into virtual reality education or VR-ed.

Food domes are needed around the world, when our weather pattern becomes unpredictable in the future. In spite of highly developed computer systems, we may need more time to research and develop this technology. Once food domes are established in the market, we will be half way toward cutting that umbilical cord with Mother Nature.

GLOBALLY EXPANDING MARKETS

If you closely observe the current level of globalization happening around the world from perspectives of both "growing market size" and "increased outsourcing," it is putting lot of pressure on the REL resources that we discussed earlier. The following diagram shows how outsourcing is easing the bottleneck of expensive labor and is further expanding the market size.

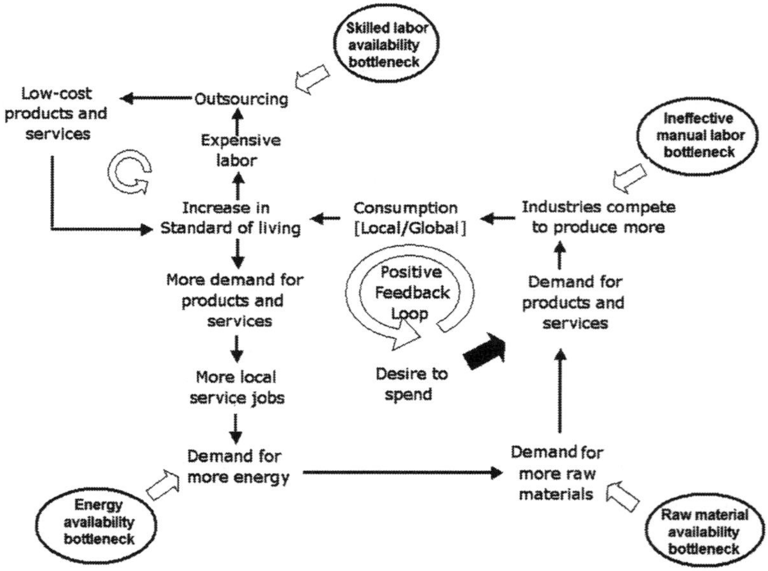

Fig 30: Outsourcing and its Effect on Global Markets

The following diagram shows how automation brings that needed relief as we move into the future.

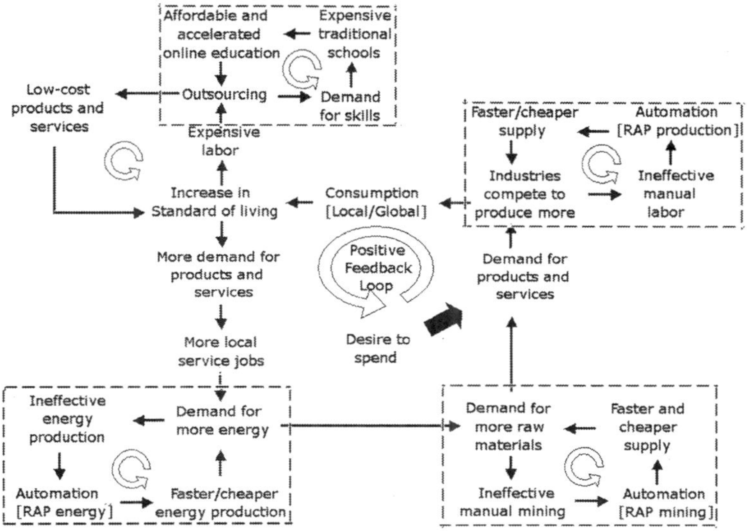

Fig 31: Automation Solutions to Eliminate Bottlenecks

The following diagram shows how automation creates the global demand for skilled labor.

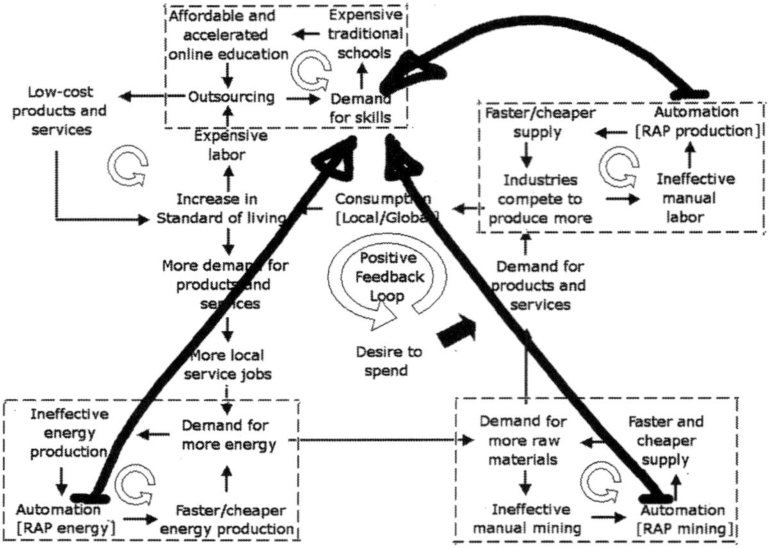

Fig 32: IROOF Solutions Requiring Mutual Outsourcing

In the diagram above, it appears as though it's "automation" holding us back from moving forward at a quicker pace. Whether it is energy, raw material, or production of goods and services, it is automation that will bring the speed needed to move forward. Automation needs a very highly skilled labor force that our current education system is not producing quickly enough. This puts pressure on the global skill demand and eventually online education takes shape not only to make education cheaper but to produce the needed skilled force at a faster pace.

LEADING THE WORLD WITH AUTOMATION

Higher skill level among the local population helps developed countries to stay ahead of the world in this hi-tech race. If a majority of a nation's population is highly skilled, automation will happen early. However, a skilled labor force will not emerge unless there is a significant demand. This becomes a chicken-or-the egg scenario. Automation will happen only if there is an ample skilled labor force, and a skilled labor force will only emerge if there are job opportunities. If we let this go on its own, the skill level gradually increases and automation will eventually happen. However, it is a slow process.

With the current limited availability of highly skilled labor, automation can be best jump-started in the energy sector. Once the RAP technology matures, other industries will start adapting RAP in their own manufacturing processes. When the demand for skilled labor increases, the current education system will undergo changes and will go online to bring down the cost of education and to produce skilled labor quickly enough to feed the fast growing market.

Therefore, the responsibility of jump-starting automation falls on the energy sector as well as academic institutions. The responsibility of educational systems is to bring down the cost of quality education, to teach more of the global population, and to adapt "accelerated" learning to match the market demand. The responsibility of energy producing companies is to adapt automation as much as the skilled labor force allows them to, so that there is always demand for skilled labor in the market. It all comes down to producing, and utilizing skilled labor to move towards automation. This is how we have grown all these centuries and this is how we will continue to grow.

PRACTICING THE ART

Here is how we all can contribute to the global growth. If you are in school, plan your career after considering the effects of both globalization and automation. Every job faces global competition in the future. Remember, if they cannot be outsourced, they eventually will be automated. Automation happens at a much higher pace in developed countries than in underdeveloped ones. No matter which part of the world you live in, you need to consider both aspects for career planning.

If you are planning to drop out of school, think again. With global competition, you will not go far. If you are dropping out because of financial reasons, a likely scenario for many, consider online training. Online institutions are the future of education system and you will see a surge of activity in the near future.

If you are in college, make sure you learn cutting edge technology to begin your career. Globalization is a rapid growth and affects all industries. Anticipating the changes well ahead and continuous training are the key elements to keep your job. No matter how current your skills are and what cutting edge technology you have acquired, they change over time. It is not uncommon to see people laid off as the economy fluctuates. If you are keeping up your skills, finding another job will not be a problem. In the future, this pressure will be much greater.

If you are already in the work force, the awareness of future automation will not only make you proactive at work, but also make you an asset to the company. Be ready for changes in your workplace, as competition between companies grows more intense in the future. You will be much better off if you can anticipate those changes yourself rather than being surprised when they happen. All these years, changes in the workplace used to happen on a very gradual pace. Now, because of the surge in globalization, changes are happening drastically and we need to understand the necessity to plan ahead. Well-informed employees are a boon to organizations when such changes happen. We have seen in many organizations, employees resisting changes. They want to do things the way they have always been done. This puts a restriction on the organization's growth and in turn human technological development as a whole. Both the organization and the employees should understand the evolutionary path the world is treading.

If you are a parent, the knowledge of The Art of Looking into the Future helps you guide your children in the right direction. Let your children know how your own job is changing, what kind of global competition you are facing in your own career, and what have you planned to face it. This will help your children understand the technological evolution you are going through and what they can anticipate in their career.

If you are retired, this is a great time to open a dialogue with your friends to figure out what the future will look like. Try applying the five principles discussed in this book to the career you have just retired from and see how they changed over time and how the jobs will be different in the future. You will become a well-informed guide to your children and grandchildren in planning their future.

If you are a philanthropist, you can help the world by promoting **online** education centers in underdeveloped countries. Remember, the more children you enroll into the education system the less violence there will be in the world. While you enjoy the ethical satisfaction of educating world children, the world enjoys the little push you gave for the global economic growth.

MOVING OUT OF RECESSION WITH RAP

If you look at today's unemployment rate in the United States, it is the highest in decades. This is mainly because of the economic slow down. Most logical way to accelerate the creation of more jobs is to increase our market size, which in turn will open up more industries. To increase the market size, people have to buy more goods and services. People will buy/invest more if they have confidence in the economic growth. The lack of consumer confidence has caused our current economy to stagnate. While it will eventually pick up its lost momentum, recovery is a slow process.

Now the quicker solution is, without relying on outsourcing, we can bring down the cost of products and services by reducing the cost of energy with RAP. As discussed earlier, when energy prices come down, it reduces the cost of raw materials. With cheap products and services the market quickly expands. More industries open up creating new jobs.

RAP creates more local jobs, especially in the research, design, and maintenance of automated machines. These jobs cannot be outsourced, although the manufacture of machine parts and assembly of machines and robots can be. For example, automating the textile industries would create more local design, development, management, and maintenance jobs. Only machine assembly work would be outsourced.

Whenever the economy bounces back, it will need more energy to sustain and grow. It is not getting the economy to bounce back that is important; but how to sustain this energy-hungry monster in the future. If a sufficient energy supply is not in place, we will begin to face more frequent recessions in the future.

Remember, it is energy that will accelerate our technological growth; it is energy that will make us stronger in the future. It is energy that can bring us out of recession more quickly than any other means. Promoting RAP to produce energy is the quickest way to create jobs.

PART IV

The Long Awaited Automation Age

IN THIS PART:

CHAPTER 20

THE INEVITABLE AUTOMATION

Decades ago, long before industrialization, our technology was so naive most products were produced manually. The best place to get a feel for the manual labor era is an antique shop. Every utensil and every consumable product, from cloths to medical equipment, was made by hand. The quality of these products reflects the standard of living. For instance, manual weaving was so slow clothes were not only expensive, but there was little variety. People were not able to afford new clothes until the old ones were worn out. That is how it became customary in many countries to buy and wear new cloths during special occasions. The current textile machines that replaced human labor have improved manufacturing capacity to such an extent, clothes are not only affordable but the varieties are plentiful.

The same argument can be applied to every other product. One hat per person, one pen per person, or one pair of shoes per person, was the norm in those days for ordinary people, although the rich had a different lifestyle. In olden days, even the transportation was so slow it would take days to travel from one city to another. Even the houses people lived in were basic, without any modern day luxuries.

Compare all of that to our current automation. Even though current production methods are only partially automated, there are more varieties, better quality, and more affordable products. If we go on listing each item we had then, compared to what we have now, we will see a pattern of machine-supported lifestyle. Day after day, automation is creeping into our lives. The driving force is our own desire for better living.

The two diagrams below show the two scenarios.

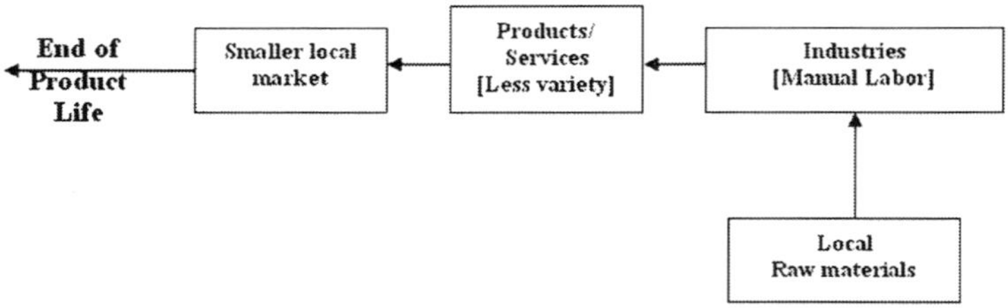

Fig 33: Past Industrial Development with Manual Labor

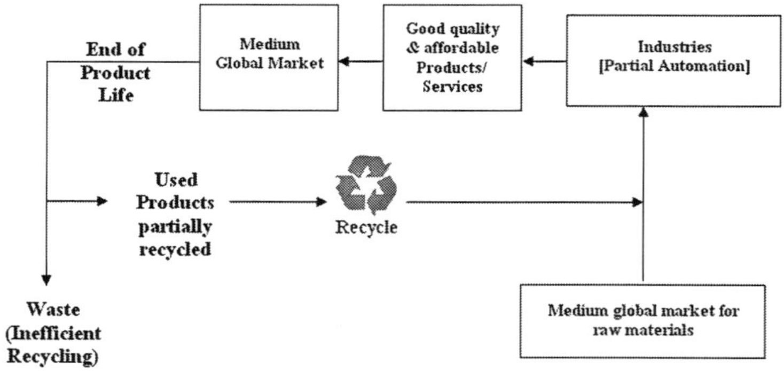

Fig 34: Current Industrial Development with Partial Automation

If you look at the above two scenarios, what is happening in reality is a systematic transfer of work to machines. "Weak human body, but amazing mind." This is the basis of automation. Humans by nature are intelligent enough to build tools and machines to do hard jobs. It is an intelligent species in the process of evolution. Eventually, humans will stop using muscle power to produce products or offer services. Instead, they will use their intellect to develop sophisticated machines to do manual jobs. Every machine is a piece of our own intellect.

Automation is always occurring in all industries no matter how small it is. To recognize this automation, we need to trace it through its history. Be it a food chain or a car manufacturer, if you look at the company's history, or even just flip through their archived photos, you can see the automation they have gone thru. Every industry has gone thru this machine-supported development. The diagram below shows the anticipated future industrial development with full automation.

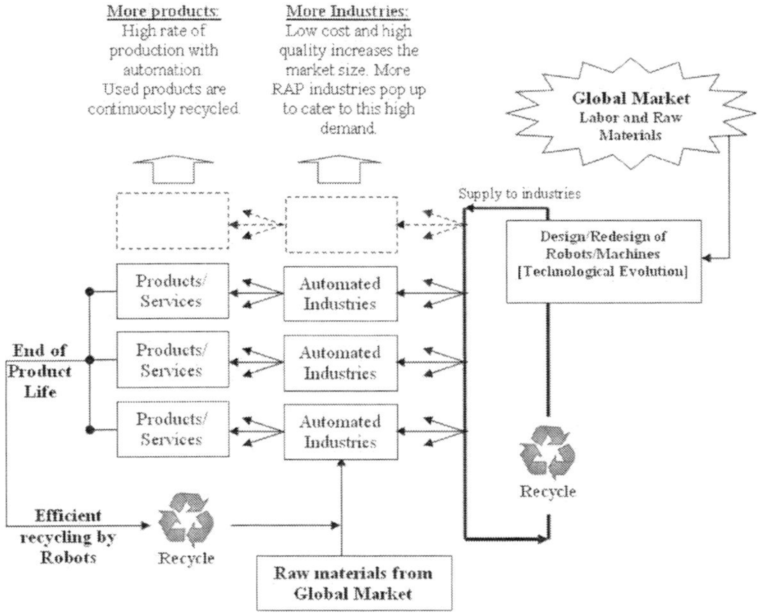

Fig 35: Future Industrial Development with Full Automation

The above diagram shows a very generic representation of the Age of Automation. Industries may either do their own research and development to build machines for automation or they may buy machines from other companies that produce them.

With energy prices at rock bottom, fully automated industries, and free recyclable raw materials efficiently collected by robots, because of efficient **RAP** mining, a machine economy will raise the standard of living to an unimaginable level.

In the Age of Automation, employees will continue to work the same nine to five jobs, but to manage machines instead of manual work. The machines will work 24/7 and produce high quality, low cost products for us to consume. The machines will also be capable of **replicating** if the demand for products increases. In the Age of Automation, starting or expanding an existing company will be very smooth and swift, as **RAP** methodology is used by all, and the robots can easily replicate as and when needed.

You may wonder, once humankind surpasses all the current day problems and reaches a comfortable lifestyle, will technological evolution continue in the future? Our history can answer that question very well. In the past, putting food on the table was the task for the entire day. Today, food is not the criterion that drives us to work. We spend a half hour in a restaurant for lunch; many times we will be working while eating! Although food will suffice to survive, we never were content with just eating food. We have come a long way satisfying our desires for technological advancement, to make our lives better.

HOW RICH WILL WE BE IN THE AGE OF AUTOMATION?

We may earn the same amount of money in the Age of Automation (excluding inflationary effects), but our buying capacity will increase as prices fall. With the world population stretching into the billions, what level of automation and standard of living will we achieve?

In the Age of Automation, consumers will develop new habits. As products became low cost, new habits will be evident as we replace our personal items more often. For example, a quality laptop computer currently costs about $1,000. We typically keep them for at least three years. Now, what will happen to this scenario if, suddenly, laptops only cost $50 or less because of automation?

Suddenly, we could have a laptop in every room! Moreover, if we encountered any problem, instead of fixing the problem, we would just replace them with a new one. If a new version arrived on the market with better features, we would be inclined to buy them, as they would be very affordable.

The same argument will apply to cars. We keep them for years. What happens if a brand new car suddenly only cost $1000 or less? No one will keep them around for more than a year. In the Age of Automation, new features will come to market more frequently. Our current global economy reveals new features in every new release. We routinely look forward to seeing upgrades in newer models. Manufacturers are forced to produce better designs and quality to satisfy their customers. In the Age of Automation, we will likely replace our cars every three months, not because there is some problem, but simply because we want to enjoy all those new features just released in the market. And, at that price...why not?

Currently, good living room furniture costs about $5,000 and lasts at least five to ten years. In fact, some people keep them for even longer. What happens if, thanks to automation, the same brand new furniture costs $50? Who will keep them for a decade at those prices? We will all recycle them every year, or maybe even several times a year. Maybe, at those prices, we will buy new furniture every time we threw a party, much the same way we buy new birthday or holiday decorations. This will happen if machines take over the production and delivery of the products. Even those industries will not have to look for raw material elsewhere. They will just have to pick up the discarded furniture – which will become raw material. We will start buying and throwing things away quite often, and the industries will retrieve them and produce new ones each time with new features.

The Age of Automation, however, will not be a bed of roses. Job losses will be more rampant and more polarizing than in the current era. Almost every manual job will be at risk in both the developed and developing world.

IS AUTOMATION A BOON OR A CURSE?

Although automation or robot sourcing, causes job losses, it also simultaneously creates jobs. This concept has already been discussed under the principle of automation [Chapter 6]. Let us revisit this concept again to make it clearer.

A typical manufacturing company in a developing world that adapted **RAP** may lay off as many as 90 percent of its employees. A new **RAP** industry will hire only 10 percent of its normal work force and machines will handle the rest. These RAP industries produce more goods to feed the hungry global market – a result of the positive feedback loop of globalization discussed earlier. Remember these **RAP** industries will require machines and robots to operate. More RAP industries mean more demand for robots and other automated machineries. This constant demand will require new businesses to open up to produce machines and robots. This demand will need more workers to design and assemble those robots/machines. The laid off workers will be the first ones to be absorbed after re-training as they will have the experience in those specific industries.

For instance, take the example of road repair. As globalization has a positive impact, there will be more economic activity in major cities, more roads appearing in newer suburbs and existing roads busier. In proportion to the economic activity, the standard of living of people also increases and skilled labor become expensive. At the same time, road blockages have a negative impact on economic activity. With booming industries paying substantial taxes, the local city governments will be rich enough to have roads repaired quickly without affecting the economic activity. This is how automation takes control of the economy.

Now, say "road repair" process is automated. The existing companies design and build road repair equipment and machines that are remotely controlled. These automated machines can repair the roads as they roll on the street, without any human intervention. A considerable number of people are needed to design and assemble these machines. This opens up another fast growing industry. They hire people who have the technical knowledge of road repair. The current employees who have the knowledge are an asset to those companies to help build the machines to do all the manual work they themselves used to do.

You may argue these automated industries may not absorb all the laid-off workers in that industry. We may see machines replacing humans, but we fail to see the full impact of machine pace. When we automate any job, not only does its cost go down, the pace of production increases exponentially. Just like automating a bottling process that produces millions of bottles a day or automating a textile company producing thousands of dresses each day. The same logic is applied to road repair as well.

Once the machines are built, they are easy to replicate. They can repair thousands of roads at the same time, not one by one like is done today by blocking roads off for weeks or months. The machines not only do this job continuously without a break, but they also can be scheduled at will. You can put them on the job or take them off at your discretion. You can pull them off during peak hours and make them work at night. Once the automatic machines come to market, we will see many roads being built or repaired simultaneously on a regular basis instead of once every several years. Just imagine, a thousand machines working all night and seeing a brand new road in the morning. A pothole you spotted on one day is not seen the next day. An automatic repair machine that already scanned the road has repaired it.

As the machines are easy to replicate, there will be thousands of machines at work while we sleep. Compare that to our current road repair method – hundreds of workers struggling with old machines and at the mercy of high-speed traffic. Even traffic suffers with congestion during the repair season. Roads are blocked for months or even years.

When we look at automation, we invariably imagine machines replacing workers leading to massive job losses. In reality when a machine replaces a worker, it opens up another massive industry that manufactures the needed machines and other supporting industries. Just like ATM machines, which initially replaced a few bank tellers, it has now grown into a mega industry. Banks have also grown in number.

Automating an industry is like inflating a balloon. When any industry gets automated, it will go thru its own positive feed back loop initiated because of the reduced product cost and/or increased service efficiency. Its size keeps growing until the market is saturated to this new reduced cost and/or higher quality. This new market size is enormous compared to the market size when it was manual. The machines also keep evolving and need a host of researchers, designers and engineers to develop and maintain them. The extent to which the quality of a product or service can grow is far greater than what can be achieved by manual labor. In that sense, automation is a job creator and not a job destroyer.

Every act of automation removes the bottleneck of slow manual labor. The more hurdles we remove, the faster we move.

If we watch very closely, industries around us offer more examples on automation, although they have been partially automated. Comparing how these industries operated in the past with their operations after automation, a definite pattern emerges. Imagine what those industries would look like if we went back in time to manual operations. What would the cost of a car be if it was assembled manually? What would be the market size of such an expensive car? Imagine the effect of the negative feedback loop going back to the good old days. Automation and globalization are irreversible and are unstoppable. They seamlessly blend into our lives and we blend into them. We will notice their presence only when we look back at our history. Our past history has a lot to tell us. We only look at our history for facts, but we rarely look at the pattern of technological growth. If we can see what technological path are we treading, then our future will unravel itself.

After establishing the hypothesis automation is an inevitable process in our evolutionary path, let us see its consequences: the effect on **REL ((raw materials, energy, and labor))** resources.

Raw materials: In spite of recycling scrap, there will be a great demand for new raw materials in the Age of Automation. After drilling and burrowing our planet, humankind must learn eco-friendly **deep underground mining.** Without regulation and eco-friendly practices, our current mining methodology will accelerate the global warming process or bring other catastrophes.

Energy: Imagine massive **RAP** industries churning out multitudes of products on a large scale to feed the market. The demand for energy to run these machines will be sky high, requiring hundreds, even thousands of **RAP** solar power plants all over the world, built and managed by robots. For steady economic growth, the rate of producing energy should always exceed demand. Any shortage will only cause global recession. Without an eco-friendly energy resource, our current dependency on fossil fuel will accelerate the global warming process and bring frequent recessions.

Labor: With so many industries, there will be increased job opportunities globally to manage the machines. High skill level will be in great demand and our education system by then must be capable of producing the needed skilled labor force. The population of a country eventually becomes an asset and not a liability. In underdeveloped nations, often poverty is blamed on the population growth. In the Age of Automation, population fuels not only consumption but production as well and makes these nations grow faster.

With such a future scenario, long term planning should be focused on automated energy production, accelerated education and automated deep underground mining.

In the future chapters an effort has been made to give a glimpse of our fast future life. Technological advancements in some major industries have been highlighted.

CHAPTER 21

TRANSPORTATION IN THE AGE OF AUTOMATION

Introducing "Self Driving Cars"

Did you know Car-computers will be driving our cars very soon? Did you know taxis will disappear from the street altogether? In fact, very soon, we may no longer need personal cars. Instead, we will just hop into a robot-car on the street and punch in our destination.

Though most drivers are law-abiding citizens, human error is inevitable when people are distracted or stressed; accidents happen and many times, are fatal. Considering the stress we are all going through, frankly, no one wants to drive.

Before looking at the future of cars, let's see how our cars evolved all these years. If we apply the first principle to cars as a product, we notice our car industry, in general, has grown and will continue to grow, satisfying the three criteria – Invention/Evolution (I/E), Quality, and Cost.

The primary criterion for the invention of a car is "to transport." Automobile companies have designed and built varieties of vehicles – sedan, coupe, minivan, and SUV – to satisfy this desire. As the usage of cars increased over time, "safety and comfort" became evolution criteria. Many safety devices have been invented, giving rise to such features as air bags, ABS, and so on. Driving comforts have also evolved, giving rise to such features as air conditioning, power windows, power steering, cruising and so on. Without comforts modern vehicles simply would not be on the market.

As we progressed, "speed" became another evolution criterion that gave birth to all modern cars that take us from one place to another at a high speed. Though the demand for high-speed cars was always there, we could only achieve higher speed within the vehicle's stability level. Now with better technology and better roads, although we are able to achieve relatively higher speeds, human driving is simply not able to keep up with the demand. Simple mistakes lead to deadly accidents at higher speeds. Humans are not able to cope with this intense pressure while driving. No matter what safety features we have, the speed works against it. Even with the speeding ticket system, our traffic has not slowed and accidents are on the rise. Human error is the culprit behind most road accidents.

The solution to this problem is to gradually reduce and then eliminate human involvement in driving. The approach is in two phases. Building interactive cars will be the first phase and building self-driving cars will be the second phase.

PHASE-1: INTERACTIVE CARS (CAR-COMPUTER)

"Interaction" will become the next evolution criterion that will evolve our cars into the future. Cars need to "interactive" with all of their critical parts to make them more responsive and driver friendly. Critical parts include the breaking system, the ignition system, the steering system, the engine components, the transmission system, and so on. Information from these components will go into the brain of the car, the "Car-computer."

A typical Car-computer will be a high-capacity server mounted in a convenient location inside the automobile with a screen integrated into the dashboard. This Car-computer will interact with all the hardware components discussed above. An integrated Car-computer will be needed very much to bring cars to life.

Current car technology is already moving in this direction. Many car components are already in interactive mode. Many new car models indicate with warning lights or messages on dashboard if things need attention to like low tire pressure, low oil level or dirty air filter etc. Some cars also have sensors that help while reversing, parking or changing lanes.

Below is a discussion of how the same technology if grew further would help us lead a safer life.

COMPUTERIZED TRAFFIC INTERSECTIONS

In the future, all traffic intersections will have transmitters transmitting digital signals instead of just traffic lights. The Car-computer will continuously monitor and control car speed depending on the signals it receives. In essence, instead of drivers stopping the vehicles at the intersections when the traffic light turns red, the car- computer will sense the traffic signal and stop the vehicle. In fact if the transmission signals are strong enough, cars will know ahead of time, when to stop, so the breaking action will not be abrupt.

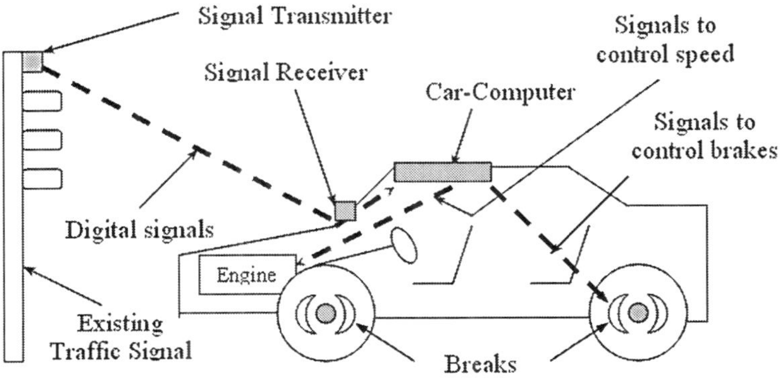

Fig 36: Computerized Traffic Intersections

This feature will not only avoid accidents at intersections, but also move traffic more efficiently. The requirement for this feature will be an enhancement to already existing traffic-sensors at the intersections to send signals to cars when the traffic light changes. The Car- computers will pick up this signal and control the vehicle speed accordingly.

If a pedestrian crosses the road in front of a moving car, the sensors placed in front and behind the car will send the information to the Car-computer and the car will stop and not move until the road is clear in front. With this feature, the driver will have less stress, as they will not have to manually control the car speed at the intersection and look out for pedestrians. Pedestrians at intersections will also feel safer. Once the feature becomes a standard feature in all cars, traffic lights will gradually cease to exist, with traffic sensors managing the traffic.

On highways, the same feature will control the speed of moving vehicles, automatically adjusting to the designated speed on the highway. Transmitters placed on highways at specific places will transmit that information to Car-computers. GPS satellites can also be used to send this information to avoid the dependency on, and the cost of producing and maintaining, road signs. These features in cars will eliminate rash driving on highways. Even the police could remotely control the speed and stop a specific car, if needed. This will put an end to dangerous high-speed car chases we hear about on roads today.

PHASE-2: SELF-DRIVING CARS

In bigger cities, it is not uncommon to see some car companies researching and even taking their self-driving cars to test-drive. From an evolutionary angle, self-driving technology will emerge when the three **"automation forces"—L**ess effective manual work, **E**xpensive labor (driving in this case), and availability of **T**echnology—come together.

It is also not uncommon to see some people openly expressing their concern about the safety and reliability of such a technology. The truth is self-driving autos are much safer than human driven cars, as there is no manual error. The following discussion will show us how such a technology could evolve.

The Car-computer discussed above will gradually evolve to take over driving responsibilities as well. The main feature needed for the car computer to drive on its own is the generation of a virtual lane. To generate this virtual lane, it could use signals from roadside transmitters, signals from other car transmitters, its own sensors and radars, signals from commercial GPS, and so on. How all these various devices come together depends on the results of the research going on around the world today. The point is, the Car-computer can safely, and securely, drive on the generated virtual lanes. They could overtake other slow moving vehicles with ease by using digital information. Suddenly, where driver-error once made interstates a dangerous way to travel, highways would become the safest place to travel.

If an entire road was damaged or flooded, then the Car-computer will alert the driver several miles in advance. If the driver does not start to manually steer, the car will automatically pull over to the shoulder of the road and stop before reaching the damaged site. At that point, the driver can take over and steer manually.

While self-driving works very well inside cities, the long drives between cities may follow a different technology. Even though robot-cars are comfy, safe, and secure, they are not meant for high-speed travel. Higher speeds always work against safety. For long distance travels, new technologies like high-speed "levitation" trains, which not only carry passengers but also carry passenger cars may emerge. Commuters can call a robot-car, put in all their belongings, drive to, and park in these fast trains. Traveling to the next city will take minutes rather than several hours.

The busier we get, the faster speeds we'll need. However, speed beyond a certain upper point is difficult for these trains to achieve because of air resistance. Reduced-pressure tubes in which trains can move at ultra-high speeds could eliminate this problem. When that becomes a reality, there will be more demand for land travel than air travel, as average train speed will be much higher than average speed of airplanes. Air travel however will still be used for flying overseas.

LIFESTYLE CHANGES WITH ROBOT-CARS

Self-driving cars will dramatically change our way of living. As no drivers will be needed, manned taxis will become obsolete. Driverless taxis will become so inexpensive people will use them for daily transportation rather than buying their own cars. Automakers will build these self-driving cars or **"robot-cars"** instead of individual cars and run them on roads, which will quickly transform into a service industry.

Robot-cars will always be available on the street in any part of the city. We might no longer need personal cars but instead, we will just hop into a robot-car and enter our destination. This will be a big relief from car ownership and maintenance chores! Car-manufacturing companies will compete with each other to provide state of the art cars on the roads for people to hire.

As traffic will be completely controlled by computers, it will be highly predictable. They will even predict traffic before it happened, as traffic monitoring devices will have the history of all car movements. Many employees go to the office and back home in a very predictable fashion. When people punch in their destination, the Car-computers will reroute traffic to alternate less busy routes without human intervention.

In city areas where there are innumerable traffic signals, the Car-computers will reroute the cars where there is less traffic. This will make the intersections less congested.

Now, with these robot-cars, people may not need parking spots any more. As there is no car ownership, there is no need to park cars. However, for people carrying their personal belongings may need some temporary parking. It means that the parking system will not completely go away, but will substantially reduce in size.

DYNAMIC LANES

Many times, while driving on highways, we see the other side either clogged or with relatively less traffic. This is because the lanes are fixed and are not dynamically usable. To this point, we have addressed the issue by introducing express lanes, which are often empty or inefficiently used. All this will change when Car-computers start driving our cars. Fixed lanes will become outdated. Lanes will become interchangeable dynamically and give more room to congested traffic. For instance if there are four lanes north bound and four lanes south bound on a highway, and the north bound lanes are more congested than south bound, then automatically, the robot-cars will start reducing the number of lanes going south and increase the lanes for north bound traffic.

DELIVERY ROBOT-CARS

Delivery robot-cars will be the extended tentacles of the robot malls to satisfy our desire for a fast life. When self-driving cars flood the market, they will offer other services as well. Delivery service will be the first one to go automatic. All items our home manager orders will be delivered to our homes via delivery robots. This will make our current system of manual trucking and delivery services obsolete.

AUTOMATED ROAD REPAIR

In big cities, traffic congestion because of road repair puts a lot of stress on daily commuters. Getting from one place to another is frustrating at best, and miserable and exhausting during peak hours.

Automation in road repair will emerge when the three **"automation forces"**– **L**ess effective manual work, **E**xpensive labor, and availability of **T**echnology – come together.

This requires sophisticated machines for road repair and maintenance. This is an expensive and time consuming task and will not happen overnight without private companies' involvement and motivation to invest money into improving the current machines.

One of the workable approaches will be to include a "time" factor while awarding contracts to road repair. Road maintenance contractors will not be allowed to block the roads for repair for prolonged periods. Many similar kinds of restrictions, if imposed on contractors, will create a huge demand for smart machines. This will set an environment for inventions. Businesses will compete to produce better machines and robotic road repair machines will eventually surface.

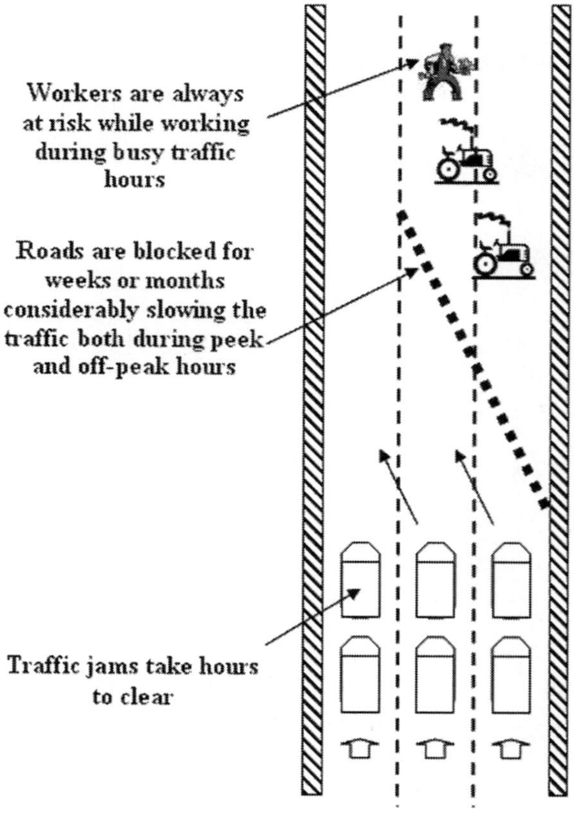

Fig 37: Manual Road Repair and Road Blocks

These compact machines will have all the road-laying ability embedded in them and they can repair or re-resurface the road as they move. The machine operators will be able to manage them remotely and safely rather than be exposed to dangerous traffic. The diagram shows the effect of roadblocks in today's traffic.

As you can see, the effect of road repair on the daily commute, especially during peak hours is not only a waste of precious time, but also exposes workers to dangerous traffic. In today's fast world, this age-old method is simply not acceptable.

The diagram below shows the effect of robotic road-repair machines on both the safety of the workers and the efficiency of work.

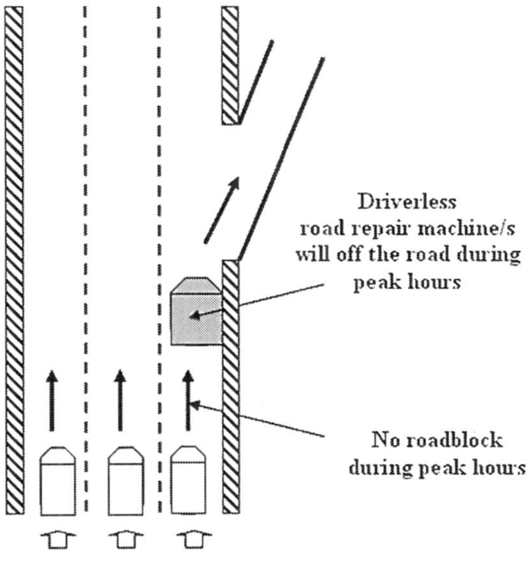

Fig 38: Automated Road Repair

The great benefit of these automated machines will be the ability to exit the road when traffic is heavy. As the repair will be done as the machine moves, there will be no road blockage and minimal impact on traffic.

Once these robotic machines are built, they are easy to replicate. Just imagine, a thousand machines working all night and seeing a brand new road in the morning. A pothole you spotted on one day is not seen the next day. An automatic repair machine that already scanned the road has repaired it.

Compare this kind of robotic scenario to our current road repair method – hundreds of workers struggling with old machines and at the mercy of high-speed traffic.

As manual labor is ineffective and technology is already available, it will not be a surprise to see robotic-road repair machines in the very near future.

CHAPTER 22

THE FOOD INDUSTRY IN THE AGE OF AUTOMATION

RAP-RESTAURANTS

While the evolution of restaurants was discussed in detail in Part I, here we discuss how the automation happens in the food preparation and how the kitchen evolves as a product.

While our current sophisticated cooking appliances are focused on saving time and improved quality, in the Age of Automation, future advances will give rise to a fully functional automated kitchen machine that eliminates the need for human involvement during cooking.

Today's restaurant kitchen will go through substantial change in the Age of Automation; it will be completely managed by machines, and a design I call a "**RAP**-kitchen."

The **RAP**-kitchen will be composed of two levels. The top level will have refrigerated containers to store cut vegetables and miscellaneous grocery items and spices for cooking. This entire top level will be circular, like a turntable and extend outside the home for delivery robots to load the inventory from outside.

The second level will be where the cooking takes place, covered in glass so people could watch the cooking in action. It consists of machine controlled cooking pans of various sizes that can shake, vibrate, toss, and turn while cooking. These pans will be held in position by the machine arm. Their movements will be fully controlled by the computer chip, the brain of the **RAP**-kitchen machine. These pans receive the raw food from the top level and deliver the cooked food out. Each pan will be electrically heated with no need for a cooking range. The machine will be supplied with built in water pipes, both to supply cooking water and later on to supply high-pressure water to clean the cooking surface.

These pans will be embedded with sensors to monitor the temperature, cooking status, food quality, and so on. The pans communicate with each other and with the cooking software. The number of pans involved in cooking, their temperature, and in what order the cooking is done will all be controlled by the cooking software, which will send signals to the computer chip. The cooking software will control the quantity of the ingredients flowing from the grocery and vegetable containers to the pans. The machine's software converts "recipe" into machine language, executing the jobs in successive order.

Thousands of cooking recipes can be stored in this machine and thousands more could be downloaded from the Internet as meals are ordered. Just choose the item from the menu and order it electronically from the very table you are sitting. There is no need for a waiter to take your order. The machine will cook chef-quality food at machine speed and efficiency. In addition, depending on your health needs, the RAP-kitchen will suggest certain recipes or avoid specific ingredients.

Depending on the customer usage and order pattern, the machine will order vegetables and groceries needed on a regular weekly schedule. If a specific food is needed for a party and if ordered in advance, the machine will be ready to dish out the food.

Delivery robots will load groceries and vegetables into the kitchen machine from the outside. Restaurant manager have no major role in maintaining the daily grocery inventory at all. Everything is taken care of by the machines, saving hours of time, producing a great meal every time.

Though this may sound futuristic today and one wonders whether such a kitchen machine will ever evolve, our lifestyle is changing and there is a very high probability that such a machine will emerge from our own desire to save time and to achieve high quality, low cost and great food varieties it offers.

The only bottleneck that would slow down the evolution of such a machine might be the food scanning technology that can scan the food being served for any spoiled food residues.

AGRICULTURE IN THE AGE OF AUTOMATION:

-The Creation of Artificial Biosphere

In the Age of Automation, agriculture will be forced to go robotic based on the principle of automation as manual labor becomes very expensive or unavailable. The need for high quality, low cost food will make the world move in this direction.

Global warming effects will also boost the growth of existing technology behind artificial biospheres to survive in extreme weather.

In the future, an artificial biosphere will be robotically managed, tall multi-floor glass structures that grow crops any time during the year, regardless of the season. Improving significantly on Mother Nature, this computer-controlled biosphere will create exactly the environment needed for a specific crop.

The biggest challenge for the invention and evolution of these artificial biospheres will be the enormous amount of energy needed to build and manage these agri-factories.

Once developed, these automatic machines will grow the crop ordered, regardless of outside weather conditions or time of year depending on the regional need and advance orders. Once the crop is ready, resident robotic machines will cut the crop, clean and pack it for transport. Transportation robots will transport it to the local warehouses and then to kitchen-machines. The entire agricultural cycle will become a machine affair in the Age of Automation.

As RAP technology matures, these biospheres will be built by robots in any part of the world, making the food very cheap and organic.

For this to become a reality in the Age of Automation, the research and design of such biospheres should begin in the current age. When we encounter severe climate changes and when seasons start overlapping due to global warming, natural agriculture will become impossible. Biospheres will be our only food supply when the globally warmed earth starts destroying the very plants and animals that it created.

CHAPTER 23

HOMES IN THE AGE OF AUTOMATION

What if I told you a house that once took months to build could be constructed in days, or even hours? Our next evolutionary path, the Age of Automation, will find us building mega cities in months, maybe even weeks, as opposed to decades or centuries as in the past.

Applying the principles of evolution to "home" as a product, we find as an evolutionary product, it has evolved satisfying all three criteria: Invention/Evolution (I/E), Quality, and Cost. Though the invention criterion of home has been "to shelter" from wild nature, "comfort" soon became the evolution criterion. This criterion drove the evolution of homes for centuries. Our modern homes look pretty much like mini factories with all the heating, refrigeration, ductwork, pipes, wires, and so on. With that kind of sophistication, and with so many man-hours going into them, no wonder modern homes are so expensive.

Recently "safety and security" has become another major evolution criterion. In the past, for security, people used just locks on their doors. Over time, this evolution criterion has evolved into full time home security monitoring. Most of our modern homes are designed to handle all aspects of "safety and security" including theft, CO monitoring, flood, and so on. When people look at buying homes, they look at all the comforts it has to offer and its ability to provide security.

Though competition is holding construction costs down, technology is gradually pushing the cost upward. Skills like carpentry, plumbing, and electrical work are highly paid because of the technology involved in handling the sophisticated machinery, which includes both tools and the appliances. This technology driven industry will become more expensive in the future. Until we move out of manual labor and skill-dependent industries, there is no reason for home construction cost to come down.

In today's world, land cost is much more than construction cost in some prime localities. This land cost however will decrease noticeably in the future as we begin to find technologies that speed up our transportation.

Now lets discuss the effect of automation on home construction. The home building industry in the United States and other developed countries has focused on wood as the primary building material. In years past, wood was not only very cheap, but easy to handle. It had a number of good qualities required of a home building material. It has remained an unchallenged resource even today. Just like oil and coal, which dominated the energy industry, wood dominates the housing industry. All the technological evolution naturally has gone in that direction. Unfortunately, we realized a little late that wood was the wrong choice, as it leads to deforestation and a resource bottleneck for the industry. Wood is **not** a strong enough material to withstand the wild effects of global warming. The difficulty in moving away from this resource is thousands of industries have already been well established in the market with millions of workers engaged in it.

We must start now to shift this dependency to a more eco-friendly source. In the future, with increased population, the demand for homes will grow so much all the forests put together will not be enough to meet the demand. With a high standard of living, there is every chance the world population will grow considerably faster. Considering the rate at which our cities are growing, these days are not far away.

With the effects of global warming, we may need to build cities not in years, but in days as global warming threatens land life. With all these future problems, we need to find a reliable resource that suits future requirements. This resource should be easy for automated machines to manage using **RAP** methodology. It should also be abundantly available throughout the world, moving away from dependency on forests and strong enough to withstand global warming. What is the probability of finding a raw material that has these good qualities?

The most obvious raw material is soil mixed with appropriate binding ingredients. It is already a major building material in many countries. **RAP** could be used to automate home construction using this material. It also could be made very strong by mixing with other cementing materials. Unfortunately, the technology has not grown around this material enough to quickly adopt it, although, it would be worth making that move. An effort has been made below to show how we could adapt soil in home building with **RAP**.

In this very likely automation scenario, a huge home building machine will roll onto the street in question, arrive at the construction site, and dig the soil out in minutes – instead of days – to form a pit that will become the foundation as well as basement for the home. The machine will then place a pre-fabricated, hi-tech, metal skeleton, the shape and size of which will match with the home plan that has been chosen by the homeowner. This skeleton will be transported in a collapsed state and expanded at the site. I call this a hi-tech skeleton, as it will have numerous sensors to monitor pressure, temperature, stress, and strain during its entire life as a supporting structure. It also interacts with house building software exchanging digital information.

The machine will then mix the excavated soil with other clay like cementing materials and spray the resulting slurry with the robotic arms onto the skeleton both from inside and out. The sprayed surface will be scanned for any unevenness and repeated coats be sprayed until the wall is smooth and thick enough, as per the design. The metal skeleton eventually will become the reinforcement to the building.

In another scenario, instead of using a prefabricated metal skeleton, molten metal will be extruded on site to form the skeleton and then the robotic arms will spray the slurry as described above. If we go on listing all possible ways, we could find many different ways of creating this raw structure for a home.

Once the structure is ready, the entire house will be heated to several hundred degrees, so the house's inside walls will become a smooth glossy surface without any need for further painting. The house exterior will have a brick finish that is hard and strong to withstand the harshest climate. More research is needed to find the best combination of ingredients to achieve the desired qualities.

Once the structure is completed, all the fixtures, including heating, air conditioning, washing machines, and even the refrigerators are just screw-on items from the outside instead of inside of the house. This will make it easy for robots to replace them from outside when needed. Every one of these appliances will be interactive, sending signals when they needed servicing. The "home manager" software (which will be discussed later) will then pick up the signals.

As technology improves, we will find ways to change wall color digitally to satisfy the desire for choices in wall colors and walls will have digital paintings.

Using the embedded digital sensors, the health of the house structure will be monitored by computers. If there was a water leakage or fire in the house, the sensors will pick it up instantly and attend to it even before you knew it.

Crawling mouse-sized robot-cleaners will keep the house clean. With the advanced technology readily present in the Age of Automation, every electric device in the house will have its own energy source, making external power unnecessary. Vacuum drying and burning the sewage eliminates the need for disposing sewage via pipe. The only outlets to the outside world will be, in fact, for water, which also could be recycled as our technology improves. This kind of self-contained technology will be very handy as we break the umbilical cord with nature. In the future, living an eco-free life will mean no help from Mother Nature to clean up after us.

These RAP houses will be stronger than the man-made wooden counterparts. They also would be easily demolished and rebuilt quickly. The down side is these home building machines will be huge and consume a lot of energy. However, after adapting **RAP** methodology in our energy sectors, energy will be very affordable and these mega projects will become more practical and very affordable.

In the Age of Automation, using the **RAP** concept in building our residential homes, and soil as main raw material, will move us away from dependency on forests. As the technology matures, competition will produce stronger and cheaper houses. At that time, we will see a house being built in a matter of hours versus a matter of months or years. The **RAP** concept described above is just an example to show how better, stronger, and cheaper homes can be built.

In the scenarios above, **RAP** will eliminate a huge bottleneck of manual labor that not only makes the houses more expensive but also slows our progress. It is not necessary the details above be followed exactly by the industry. In all honesty, the methods employed can be far different to suit the economic and technological capability available at that time.

RAP-KITCHEN IN HOMES

In the Age of Automation, as people become busier with work, daily cooking at home becomes more of a hassle. Our dependency on canned and frozen food will continue to increase. However, human desire for freshly cooked food will never diminish. The good news is that automation offers alternative solutions for the busy life style. The RAP-kitchen that began to evolve in restaurants will find its way in homes too but in a much smaller version. For larger family sizes, home kitchen becomes a necessity, as it is a great time saver. In future homes, unlike any other appliances, home kitchen becomes a key appliance that greatly increases the standard of living.

Thousands of worldwide recipes can be stored in this machine and thousands more could be downloaded from the Internet as and when needed. Just choose the recipe and the machine will cook chef quality food. Meals will be categorized much like a song play list on your computer – by weekday, holiday, time of day, time of year, food groups, or even family members' favorite recipes.

If you select the menu ahead for an entire week, the machine will order any additional ingredients needed in advance. If you plan a weekend party, the machine will be ready to dish out the food. In addition, depending on your health needs, the RAP-kitchen will suggest certain recipes or avoid specific ingredients.

Delivery robots will load groceries and vegetables into your kitchen machine from the outside. As a homeowner, you will have no regular involvement in maintaining the grocery inventory at all. Everything is taken care of by the machines, saving you hours of time, producing a great meal every time.

Home version of RAP-kitchen will emerge from our own desire for good life style and food varieties it offers and of course to save precious time.

Though the home RAP-kitchen will be meant to cook our food that is consumed on a daily basis, restaurants will use similar machines, only on a larger scale, to handle many different recipes as they can store rare ingredients too.

Chefs will continue to create new recipes that are better tasting and healthier to suite the evolving human lifestyle. Television channels showing food preparation will become much more popular, as it will be easy to prepare them with machines rather than rely on our own skills. Today, when we watch a food channel and try to cook the same food, many times we do not even come close to the chef's quality. With RAP-kitchen, you will simply punch in a code on your machine, the recipe will be downloaded, and you will enjoy chef's quality food.

However, the limitation though to this kitchen machine is it could not do anything more than what it was designed to do. If the machine could not execute some jobs that were in the recipe or did not find the specified ingredient, then it will be rejected or an alternate recipe will be generated, depending on user choice. These limitations will be addressed as the machine advances. This is what technological evolution is all about – machines adapting to human needs.

MEET YOUR HOME MANAGER

As we become comfortable with technology, managing our busy lifestyles with timesaving features in our homes becomes exceedingly important. The need for a computer controlled home becomes inevitable.

In such a home, all home appliances must be interactive, linked electronically to a home-management software program, designed to understand our habits and maintain our homes accordingly. The home manager software will control kitchen appliances, laundry machines, robotic home-cleaning machines, heating and cooling devices, security cameras, fire extinguishers and a host of other appliances.

In the event of a fire, for instance, the home manager will identify the exact spot via temperature sensors and video cameras and will put out the fire via fire extinguishers located around the house for this purpose, even before fire engine arrive.

The home manager will do routine chores such as ordering personal inventory, grocery and personal items. The manager will report malfunctioning appliances to the dealers who will replace them robotically, and will even vacuum the floor via crawling micro-robots. The list of services is nearly endless.

Just imagine the time it will save us. How will the computer know when to place an order for inventories in homes? In a typical home, items to be monitored by the Home Manager will be placed in specific containers with sensors to detect usage. After a few weeks, the computer will detect a pattern to our habits and maintain the inventory accordingly.

CHAPTER 24

LIVING IN THE AGE OF AUTOMATION

HEALTHCARE IN THE AGE OF AUTOMATION

What will life be like beyond the home in the Age of Automation? The same technology, innovation, and convenience that mark self-driving cars and home managers will make life beyond our personal homes and vehicles an equally miraculous and functional place.

In the Age of Automation, healthcare will become more precise and dependable. Our heath will be a top priority to health insurance companies, reducing the cost of treating diseases later on.

Corrective or emergency surgery will go a step further to become preventative. Nanotechnology will evolve further to support machine managed healthcare. Machines and robots will not wait until disease or infirmity robs us of our health; instead, they will treat the disease at its onset. It will be common to see body scanners and blood chemistry health monitors placed in locations we visit regularly, be it a gym or a super market.

We are already using pills that scan our GI system, the same technology will advance and people will be using it on a weekly or monthly basis so the data is recorded and evaluated by the software on a regular basis. Any discrepancy will be attended to.

Many such real time health monitoring systems will evolve from the research desks. Insurance companies will invest heavily in such devices in the future. Though their focus is to save money, the patients will be greatly benefited.

In fact, the entire human body will be monitored like never before. You will never see a patient arriving in a hospital with arteries blocked from fat or with advanced cancer. Surgery will become very rare except to treat accident victims and abnormalities. At last, thanks to machine-managed healthcare, the human body will be cared for the way it should be.

In the Age of Automation, a human will get the best diagnosis and the best medicine available on the planet, no matter in which part of the world they may be living.

EDUCATION IN THE AGE OF AUTOMATION

In the Age of Automation, virtual reality will take education to a completely new level, making it available to the entire world at an affordable cost. In fact, it will become the most dominant form of media on the planet. Kids will love virtual reality education (VR-ed). Schools and colleges will use it to take the students around the world virtually.

The difference in VR-ed technology is images will **not** be computer generated, but use real images and videos shot specifically for this purpose. The concept of a multidimensional video will be used in these devices. A VR-ed generator will not be just one camera, but rather a set of several cameras. It will look like a helmet with many high-resolution cameras fixed on it. As the videographer moves around, the cameras in the helmet shoot in a million directions. When it comes to the end user, when the student wears the VR-ed device, they will turn their head as if looking around in real time. While this is simply a concept to show the possibilities of VR-ed, it will be more effective than mere computer generated images.

For instance, as a videographer walks on say London Bridge, the end users sitting in the comforts of their home, will see everything in real time from this helmet. As cameras are further miniaturized, small flying robotic bees with miniature camera eyes will fly around tourist attractions! This will be a significant milestone in tourism industry. A tourism company, for instance, can send a thousand such robotic bees to fly all over Niagara Falls, incorporate that into the VR-ed, and sell it to the public. People will buy these devices to watch the world in real time from the comforts of their homes. This example shows how VR-ed could be used by both the education and tourism industries to learn about real world experiences without physically being there.

These highly technical devices will teach our children real world experiences from the comforts of their classrooms. Showing real facts virtually to educate children will be integral to our future education system. Students will go to forests and touch plants and animals while sitting in the VR-ed suits. They can go to far away deserts and walk on the sand; they can go under water and swim with sharks. The activities available in the VR-ed suit can be limitless.

This virtual education makes it very affordable to the whole world when it gets mass-produced for the global market. The low-cost education will mean a lot to underdeveloped countries. Students could attend any class of their choice and be competitive in the market, regardless of where they live.

In the Age of Automation, the world needs highly skilled employees to design and maintain the machines. The focus of future education will be accelerated learning in a shorter timeframe. VR-ed services will become the inevitable choice to train people quickly. Employees will have to keep learning new technologies to stay current in the changing world.

ROBOT MALLS

A visit to a shopping mall will be an entirely different experience in the Age of Automation, as there will be "push thru" counters instead of regular checkout counters. You will pick the item(s) you want inside the store, and push the cart through the checkout counter. The machines will automatically sense what you are carrying and prompt you for payment at the checkout counter. The touch screen samples your DNA or scans your fingerprint, depending on the technology prevalent at that time, and identify you; no more swiping of cards and identify theft. Using this technology, all items taken from the mall will be automatically scanned and charged to your account. When you come out of the mall, you will just hop into any available robot-car. As you touch the "HOME" button, the car will know where you live, and you will be headed home. Life will be so easy and comfortable you will wonder how people used to stand in long lines just to pay!

Local grocery stores will undergo massive changes. Grocery stores and vegetable markets will become little more than storage warehouses, as most of the items needed will be ordered by the home manager and delivered by robots. In fact, it will become hard to find a grocery store or vegetable market in a city.

Robots, making the products very affordable, will operate all grocery and vegetable warehouses. As fresh vegetables arrive from artificial biospheres, they will be cleaned, cut, packed, stored, and monitored for high quality until robots deliver them to our home kitchens in refrigerated containers. We can expect high machine quality and timely delivery. Food will be continuously monitored during its entire path from biospheres to our homes. Even at home, machines will monitor the food quality until it is cooked and tabled. After eating, our health monitoring devices will monitor our blood chemistry. Food and health will eventually become a machine affair in the Age of Automation. Any kind of food problem can be quickly traced back to the plant and all the machines and storage places it went through. With that kind of food management, robot-managed food industry will be much more dependable than human managed that we have today.

DNA SAMPLERS: AN END TO IDENTIFY THEFT?

When DNA technology matures, DNA scanning will become a reliable method used by law enforcement officials to identify people.

Police and other law enforcement officials will carry hand held DNA scanning devices. To identify any person, the police officers will simply touch the person with this device that will sample the DNA of the skin or hair or sweat and give identity of that person immediately.

The same technology will go into airports, shopping malls, and banks, not only to make the system more reliable but also to protect customers from identify thefts.

In our homes, DNA keys will become popular in the future. When touching the doorknob, your fingerprint will be scanned and your DNA sampled, before the door will open. In cars, start buttons, steering wheels, breath analyzers and a host of other devices will be capable of identifying the person sitting in the car – both a convenience and a security feature. The convenience is, the car will know whom to contact in case of emergency. In addition, the police will know who is traveling in which car, as all cars are robotic cars without ownership.

In the future, information flow will become so intermingled with our lives we will not live without it. From home manager to shopping malls, our identity will be digitally traceable. Even traffic signals will record our presence as our cars pass by. With so much information accessible, it will be easy to find the location of any person at any specific time of the day or night and trace back in time as well from archived databases. Law enforcement officials will easily track people's movements, a great tool to solve crimes.

While unsettling, behind the scenes our privacy will take on a new meaning. Our personal information will be available, to anyone who has access to it. With so much of personal information out there, we should be more worried about protecting it. As we move into the future, as our personal data lives in permanent databases, security becomes more important to protect our privacy.

With so much of information readily available from DNA/fingerprint scanning, will you need passports in the future to travel? Probably not. A touch is all that will be needed for the immigration officials to know who you are, where you live, and all pertinent information, including visas, needed to travel. They can even figure out your entire travel history from your childhood. As this technology spreads around the globe, the world will become a much smarter place to live.

DNA CELL PHONES: BIRTH OF VIRTUAL CELL PHONES

Future cell phones will look far different from those we have today. As finger print/DNA scanning technology becomes more advanced, it will find its way into cell phones. Future cell phones will behave more like virtual phones and touch sensitive to identify the person holding it. Every time you use your cell phone, it identifies you by fingerprint scan or DNA to activate your ability to use it. As you touch someone else's phone, it will sense your touch and become your virtual phone, acting like your phone. You will access all your favorite numbers, favorite ringing tones, and so on, on this instrument just like your phone. All your calls will be diverted to this new instrument from your old instrument. This means, no one could use your old instrument anymore posing as you. Your old instrument will do the same thing, sensing the fingerprint or DNA of that person and becomes their phone virtually. No calls could be made from your old instrument until the instrument identified the person. Interchangeability will drive the evolution of phones in the future.

In addition, on and on…

If you apply the automation and globalization principles to all our day-to-day products and services around us, you will begin to see the future, more matured, safer and smarter time to live.

The above scenarios are a just a few examples to demonstrate how the world will evolve with the machines of the future. Once we identify this model of our technological evolution, it will not be that hard to see other future possibilities of the intelligent machines. In all these scenarios, we should remember the market demand is the driving force. If there is no market, there is neither invention nor evolution.

If the economy remains strong enough, then all the technological marvels will come to our doors naturally. If on the other hand, the economy is weak, no matter how grand our ideas are and how deep our desires are, they will be just dreams. Even though humans desire a marvelous technological evolution, only a strong economy can make it happen. A closely monitored economy is the fastest way to progress.

SOFT GOVERNMENT

As we progress into the future, the way we govern a nation will undergo substantial change. Our current governing system was created centuries ago when there were not many industries around and the economy was manually manageable. With the advent of technology, industries are growing at an unprecedented pace. It has become humanly impossible to digest all the news and everything going on in the world to make proper financial decisions.

Even advisors to presidents and prime ministers around the world have a lot of information to process before giving their opinions. If the governments do not step up to this fast changing world, they will become bottlenecks to technological growth.

Inevitably, future governments will become software-supported governments where the software will give critical advice based on real time information it receives, saving human time and avoiding human error. With software-supported systems, governments will work more efficiently, giving the economy the boost they need. Learning to manage this information world with Information Technology is critical. Humans cannot manage these giant global economies without a fast flow of information, unless we are willing to accept human errors and the consequences. The responsibility to establish robust global databases and sophisticated, information processing software falls on governments. Any investment in that direction would be worth considering.

CHAPTER 25

MACHINE PAMPERED HUMANS

After having crawled out of the current slow manual age, the Age of Automation will come as a great relief to humankind. Manual labor will cease to exist by the time we reach the end of the Age of Automation. Humans achieve the real freedom of which they dreamed. Products will be manufactured, transported, and delivered to our door by robots. Our food will be prepared by robots; homes built and managed by robots; and our health will be monitored by robots. There will be no hefty mortgages to pay, no grocery shopping to do—you will not even have to drive or cook food!

Life could not be any better.

However, it will all come with a hefty price. As the demand for quality will be sky high, life will be very hectic and stressful, making the need for these highly technological products even more necessary, with less and less time to perform such motor functions ourselves.

There will be less and less human-to-human interaction in the future. We will expect more from machine-managed systems. As we deal with machine slaves the majority of the time, we will get used to expecting the best service all the time. If a product or service were ordered, the delivery time will be set not by days but by hours and minutes. Such will be the efficiency of machines. More quality, more precision, timelier service – more of everything will mold our lives.

With the majority of jobs taken over by robots, the only jobs available to humans will be robot design, robot assembly, software development for robots, and so on – all centered around machines and robots. Every specialty, including doctors, engineers, lawyers, and a host of other professionals will put their skills into computers, so machines will do their routine chores allowing the professionals to concentrate on further growth. As competition becomes intense, job stress will be equally high…, as will the rewards.

Robots will undergo continuous change and become more sophisticated as time goes by. The need for improved robots will never stop. That is what technological evolution is all about – continuous growth in technology. In the Age of Automation, robots will know so much and we will know so little we will not be able to make a living without them.

Who will be responsible for such dependency on machines? Every one of us who demands high quality and high precision will be responsible for it. Even in today's world, our dependency on computers, cell phones, televisions, and a host of other electronic gadgets is increasing every day. If we lose them, we feel their absence. The Age of Automation is no different. Machines will offer us a high quality life. It is inevitable we will follow this path.

WHAT MOTIVATES PEOPLE TO WORK IN AN AFFLUENT FUTURE?

As machines will do all the physical work in the future, humans will enjoy hi-tech houses, speedy services, healthy food, high quality healthcare and a longer life. Every dollar earned in the Age of Automation will have a higher buying capacity. People will be so well off they can vacation for years. But, will they?

Our evolutionary future looks so rich and secure one wonders if we really need to work at all in the future. Will all the comforts we get in the future make us less motivated to work? Will that be a disaster to the economy? Will we hit economic recessions and depressions in the future because of lack of motivation to work? These are all questions that naturally pose themselves as we look to a bright future.

Even in today's world, the same question intrigues us: why do rich people work? In fact, this has been a question ever since our ancient economy divided the rich and the poor.

It is understandable poor people struggle hard to make money. However, it is difficult to understand why the rich and famous, who have all the financial security in the world, work equally hard.

We witness this as we look around at our own neighborhoods. Looking at the affluent locales, where the average property value is $5 to $10 million, the people there are as busy as people living in very low-income areas. If we look at even more affluent locales, where the average property values are $10 to $20 million, they, too, are as busy as anyone else is. If you read about the lifestyles and activities of billionaires, they are even busier than all the others.

Achieving more in one's lifetime is the secret behind our evolution. A millionaire tries to add one more million to it. A billionaire tries to double it. More money, more power, more fame keeps us busy. Everyone struggles hard to acquire more of everything.

In the rich future, however, people will have a choice. They can sit doing nothing or work in a high stress job. If they sit doing nothing and depend on social security, their standard of living will not be high enough to enjoy all the great comforts of life. At the same time, they will not starve to death, but will have a life considerably better than what most on social security have today. However, they will helplessly watch others progressing in their lives, earning more money, recognition and identity, and enjoying all the great joys of what the world has to offer. How many of us are NOT willing to go down that path? Eventually desire wins.

To increase the standard of living, the common person will work harder, and that will keep our economy going. Rich people will try to increase their wealth, which will boost the economy even further.

Both rich and poor contribute to the growth of our economy. Our desire for "more" keeps us evolving technologically and this desire will exist as long as the human race exists.

CHAPTER 26

SPACE AGE COMES NATURALLY

The VR-ed suits that we discussed earlier will become a popular gadget in the tourism industry as technology evolves. There are two reasons for people opting for these virtual tours:

1. **The amount of time needed for a revisit.** Who wants to spend days traveling just to visit a museum or a monument they have already seen before? Visiting these places in a matter of minutes while staying in the comforts of their homes, that will make the VR tourism industry attractive.

2. **The thrill and safety associated with any tour.** In the comforts of our own homes, we fly over erupting volcanoes, dive deep into oceans, or wander in wild forests without being attacked by wild animals! The possibilities in these virtual worlds are truly endless; think of visiting the Seven Wonders of the World in as many days! Even elderly people and people with disabilities, will be fascinated by these machines, as they could visit places they never dreamed of going in their lifetimes, because of either health reasons or the prohibitive adventurous nature of such extensive travels. Even parents of small young children can opt for it.

As more people start using it, the industry will capture a bigger market. More revenue and competition will eventually make it more mature as a sustainable growth industry. As technology matures, the experience will become more satisfying and consumer-friendly. As people begin to taste this wonderful world of VR-ed, they will come back for more.

What is next? After peering into every conceivable nook and cranny of the world, people will naturally dream of flying around the planet and watching the blue heaven from space. Virtual space travel will become the most sought after industry in the world. As more and more companies compete, technology will get highly sophisticated. Even the common person will be sucked into this fascinating world and the tourism industry will take a different shape.

Humans will travel into space not on the backs of expensive, dangerous, and numbers-prohibitive spacecraft, but rather with VR-ed suites. They will fly to and walk in space; they will go through exciting adventures of landing on the moon, Mars, and other planets, remotely via sophisticated VR-ed machines. Again this is not computer generated virtual reality but real world videos and experiences captured by the robots designed and flown to space for the purpose. Imagine walking on Mars after coming home from the office, visiting fascinating worlds from the comforts of your homes – a true stress reliever!

Every day new adventures will be added as producing companies compete to capture this newfound market. After enjoying these out of the world virtual visits, people will soon wish they were there in space physically. People have a desire to fly in space and experience the ultimate happiness in their lives. The more they experience it from their VR-ed gadgets, the more the craze for real life experience will become more predominant, eventually taking the industry to another level. By then, the automated global industries will be technologically advanced enough and economically capable of developing affordable spacecrafts to satisfy the human desire to fly to space.

A "HICCUP" BEFORE FLYING

By the time humans reach the end of the Age of Automation, the demand for metal will be so high our planet will have been mined considerably. With so many robots and industries all around the globe, the demand for metal will be sky high. Though mining will be continuous, the demand will surpass the supply, giving rise to very efficient recycling industries. They will be so efficient they will pick up any trash you might discard and analyze it for possible renewability. Everything except biodegradable products will be immediately extracted and recycled.

Even with that kind of efficient recycling method, the demand for metal will never stop as people fly high. This shortage of raw material will put our economic growth on pause until our mining industries expand into underground robotic mining.

Robots will dig deeper mines underground without disturbing the environment at the surface. As metal reserves are depleted on the earth's surface, underground mining will become economically viable. This will bring out enormous quantities of metals, elevating the rocket manufacturing industries to new heights.

With energy prices at rock bottom, deep underground mining, and robots doing the hard manual tasks, humans will have all the wealth and ability to build sophisticated rockets for such space visits. Space flying will become more affordable over time. Rockets and space ships will start flying from every corner of the world. People will fly just as they would on any vacation trip. Flying into space, floating in space, and watching the earth from high above will become a common vacation activity in the Age of Automation.

HOW CLOSE ARE WE TO A SPACE AGE?

Space age is still a far-fetched idea. What we have achieved so far are mere experiments. A space age will happen only when the economy spreads its financial tentacles into space. When space agencies like NASA or Roscosmos launched a rocket or landed on the moon, it did not indicate the birth of space age. It only indicated the birth of space technology. A space age will happen when ordinary people are willing to put their money in space businesses by either buying services or opening private businesses. This will happen only if prices fall to become affordable to ordinary people. Affordability of space travel will be possible only after we pass through the Age of Automation where robots will make that possible. A space age looks very distant for now, as we have not passed through the Age of Automation. From our current perspective, only the Age of Automation is reachable. From the Age of Automation, a space age will be reachable. We have to climb the ladder one step at a time.

PART V

Survival From Extinction

IN THIS PART:

27. Global Warming and Human Ingenuity

CHAPTER 27

GLOBAL WARMING AND HUMAN INGENUITY

Any celestial disturbance, close to home, is an extinction threat to humankind. Meteor strikes, Gamma ray bursts, black holes – the list of catastrophes that could wipe us out is endless. However, the good news is all of these forces are highly predictable, following the laws of science. What we need is the right technology to unravel their mysteries.

While we are concerned about science's endless theories of how the world will end, with continuous technological growth, one day we will be able to predict and manipulate potential celestial threats. However, to get to these threats, before they get to us, it is a race against time. Although more time allows us to be more knowledgeable and stronger against these threats, we do not have unlimited time. Every economic slowdown works against us. **Every economic recession takes us closer to extinction.**

Global economy is the only shield that will protect us in the future. Protecting our economy is the same as protecting the human race. While we always look at the economy as a way of making quick money and spending it in our short lives, in reality, our future survival is in the hands of global economy.

Many argue research and technology will make us stronger. The truth is, our ability to use technology is as important as technology itself. For instance, if our researchers develop a technology to launch a gigantic space mission to divert an oncoming meteor on collision course with our planet, will we have the financial capability to manage such a huge mission? Only an equally huge global economy could handle it. If our global economy is weak, so are we.

Though the Age of Automation will give us the ultimate power to survive the global warming threat, how quickly we reach it determines our survival possibilities. Although the Age of Automation appears to be far off, the pace to reach it is in our own hands. If we understand the evolutionary nature of our global economy, and how fast we could grow it, the Age of Automation appears closer.

With a robust economy, nations can help each other during bad times. If a particular country were badly hit by a disaster, only an economically developed country could help them out. If all nations are weak, neither can they help each other nor can they help themselves. This gives us even more reason to continue building a robust global economy and not just individual economies.

HOW SERIOUSLY SHOULD WE CONSIDER GLOBAL WARMING?

Global warming is the century's most debated subject, mainly because of our concern for the planet and our own existence. Many strongly argue global warming is not really happening, as there is not enough evidence to prove it. The question is, do we have time to analyze all the current and prehistoric data and reach a conclusion? Do we have to wait for our ecosystem to show its ugly face and start wiping us out? If scientists do prove global warming is a real threat, how much time do we really have, to develop technologies to save ourselves? We have to grow our global economy and its technological capability at a higher pace to survive. The question now becomes: At what pace should we grow? What pace is right for us? Can we afford the luxury of a slow growth that we are currently going thru?

WHAT EXACTLY IS GLOBAL WARMING?

While lying down on a warm sunny beach and gazing at the sky above, have you ever wondered how warm it could be just a mile above? The atmospheric temperature decreases with altitude.

Only a small percentage of the air mass close to the ground is warm; the rest is bitter cold. In spite of the fact that a major chunk of our atmosphere is cold, we are still able to lead a comfortable life on the ground because of a stable atmosphere. Any disturbance to this brutally cold, but steady atmosphere will expose us to more cold. More freezing temperatures is what we can expect once we are closer to the devastating effects of global warming. Normally we imagine a warm climate when we think of global warming, but in reality it is cold that we should be concerned about. Global warming is all about a global weather disturbance due to temperature rise. The actual temperature rise may or may not be noticeable in all world regions, however its effects are devastating.

EVOLUTIONARY SOLUTION TO GLOBAL WARMING THREAT

Although global warming is clearly an extinction level threat, these disastrous effects of nature look different at different levels of our technological evolution. The severity of global warming depends on the level of technological evolution at the time the effects present themselves. For instance, in the current age, even a category 2-3 hurricane appears very powerful. Hurricanes and tornadoes have been killing humans and destroying properties every time they hit. It appears we are at the mercy of these natural forces. Ordinary effects of global warming appear very powerful in the current age.

In the Age of Automation, however, we will not feel as threatened by these effects. The monstrous machines will help us survive from the hostile environment and we will feel much safer. We will also be skillful enough to build our own **artificial world inside this natural**

world. We will not only survive, but also continue to evolve, and global weather will become inconsequential.

In a space age, these devastating effects will appear different from the comforts of our space cities; they will be nothing but great scenery. As long as our planet is safe from outside celestial disturbance, we will not interfere in its natural life. However, if we desire to live on the planet, we might even use our future sophisticated technology to restore the eco balance.

A RACE WITH GLOBAL WARMING

If global warming effects start threatening us in the current age, our economy will slow down and we will go into survival mode. Survival mode will not actually keep us alive for very long, because it will put an end to our economic growth. With a very weak global economy and severe global warming effects working against it, our survival will be at stake. Rather than playing defense and waiting for these events to happen, we should try our best to **outpace** the speed of global warming. If our progress into the Age of Automation occurs more rapidly, possibly even well before global warming begins to take effect, we will have a higher probability of survival and continued evolution.

Both global warming and our technological evolution are natural processes. We could manipulate them to our advantage. By using green technology, we may reduce the pace of global warming to some extent. Similarly, by eliminating all economic bubbles and the energy bottleneck, we can avoid economic recessions, to let our technology grow steadily.

If the global economy and global warming race side by side, a likely scenario considering the speed at which our economy is currently growing, we will be cutting it very close and taking chances with our very survival.

CONCLUSION

AN ART WE ALREADY HAVE

Not all countries are developing at the same pace. We still have poverty, hunger, and illiteracy in the world. We must realize all the present day problems will continue to be an issue until we move out of the current age.

Once poor regions of the world prosper from globalization and start leading comfortable lives, their focus will change from violent living to a safer and longer life. They become a huge market contributing substantially to the developing world.

The positive feedback loop of globalization will bring inevitable automation. However, if we let it grow on its own, it will take several decades or more, depending on the pace of global economic growth and the number of recessions we experience. If we progress slowly, not only will we remain vulnerable to extinction level threats, but we will continue to face internal conflicts. Until the world reaches the Age of Automation, the pace of technological evolution is paramount.

The Art of Looking into the Future that is built on the G-R-A-D-E principles offers us evolutionary IROOF solutions to begin the process of a high-paced global economic growth. These five principles not only help us see that distant future, but also help us reach that destination in time.

Though you may not agree to all the ideas and concepts, this book surely does one thing: It will make you look at world problems from an evolutionary angle. The concept of globalization and automation help us look at our own life changes in a different angle.

After all, The Art of Looking into the Future is an art we already have; we only need to master it.

ACKNOWLEDGEMENTS

There are several groups of people to whom I am very thankful for their help and advice. First, many thanks to Rusty Fischer whose valuable advice and organization of the chapters highlighted the principles on which the entire book is based. Many thanks to Cheryl Cook and Elandee Thompson for their feedback on the flow of the concepts. Thanks to Laurence Singer, David Hale, Kathleen Tracy, Alan Beck, Andrew Robinson and Tom Kerr for their valuable suggestions and evaluation of the book. And thanks to my family and friends for their helpful comments, advice and support.

I used a number of resources during the development stage of the book, including several government websites. I highly recommend these sites: www.House.gov, www.cbo.gov, www.eia.doe.gov, www.nasa.gov, www.imf.org, www.who.int, www.ers.usda.gov, www.oecd.org, finance.yahoo.com and www.cms.gov.

REFERENCES

1. Centers for Medicare and Medicaid Services, "National Health Expenditure Data: NHE Fact Sheet": https://www.cms.gov/NationalHealthExpendData/25_NHE_Fact_Sheet.asp

2. Congressional Budget Office - Healthcare expenditure: http://www.cbo.gov/ftpdocs/89xx/doc8947/MainText.3.1.shtml

3. Centers for Disease Control and Prevention. Chronic Disease Overview.

4. Dow Jones Reprint Solutions. http://www.djreprints.com/inkonpaper/iop-artimages.html

5. Macroeconomic Assumptions: USDA - United States Department of Agriculture http://www.ers.usda.gov/Briefing/baseline/macro.htm

6. Congress of the United States, Congressional Budget Office (January, 2008). Technological Change and the Growth of Health Care Spending. http://www.cbo.gov/ftpdocs/89xx/doc8947/MainText.3.1.shtml

7. Joint Economic Committee United States Congress, retrieved from http://www.house.gov/jec/news/Housing%20Bubble%20study.pdf

8. Financial Crisis Inquiry Commission THE MORTGAGE CRISIS -APRIL 7, 2010 http://www.fcic.gov/reports/pdfs/2010-0407-PSR_-_The_Mortgage_Crisis.pdf

9. U.S. Energy Information Administration, Department of Energy, retrieved from http://www.eia.doe.gov/emeu/aer/pdf/pages/sec11_2.pdf http://www.eia.doe.gov/emeu/aer/pdf/perspectives_2009.pdf

10. U.S. Energy Information Administration / Annual Energy Review 2009. Energy bubble before the recession. http://www.eia.doe.gov/emeu/aer/pdf/pages/sec11_14.pdf

11. NASA, "Water Vapor Confirmed as Major Player in Climate Change," retrieved from http://www.nasa.gov/topics/earth/features/vapor_warming.html

12. IMF - International Monetary Fund - World Economic Outlook-Sustaining the Recovery October 2009 - http://www.imf.org/external/pubs/ft/weo/2009/02/pdf/c1.pdf

13. Global Health workforce by density, - World Health Organization http://www.who.int/whr/2006/overview_fig6_en.pdf

14. 100 years of consumer spending – U.S. Bureau of Labor Statistics, U.S. Department of Labor http://www.bls.gov/opub/uscs/report991.pdf

15. MEASURING UP 2006 - THE NATIONAL REPORT CARD ON HIGHER EDUCATION – The National Center for Public Policy and Higher Education http://www.highereducation.org/reports/mup_06/MUP-06.pdf

16. Structure of earth. Retrieved from http://scign.jpl.nasa.gov/learn/plate1.htm

17. Earth's crust. Retrieved from http://earthquake.usgs.gov/research/structure/crust/index.php

INDEX

ABOUT THE AUTHOR

R. S. Amblee earned his master's in engineering and has been a software engineer for over twenty years. A globetrotter at heart he's traveled extensively in India, Australia, New Zealand, Southeast Asia, Europe, and North America. He lives in Chicago, Illinois with his family.

9105067R0

Made in the USA
Charleston, SC
11 August 2011